You Don't Say

How We Get Communication Wrong...
and How to Get It Right

Demetria M. McNeal

You Don't Say: How We Get Communication Wrong ... and How to Get It Right
Copyright © 2022 by Demetria M. McNeal, Ph. D.
All Rights Reserved

Published by
Munn Avenue Press
300 Main Street, Ste 21
Madison, NJ 07940
MunnAvenuePress.com

Paperback ISBN: 979-8-9861680-4-3

Printed in the United States of America

DEDICATION

*To all the friends who have lived life with me and who form
the foundation for this incredible work.*

ACKNOWLEDGMENTS

I want to give heartfelt thanks to the following people, whom I enjoy and respect, for making it possible for me to create this wonderful work to share with the world.

First and foremost, thank you to my husband, Andre, and bonus daughter, Adrianna, who have been with me along this journey. You have given me the adventure of being a wife and of motherhood.

To Dawn Josephson, my writing coach and editor extraordinaire, who believed in the book from the beginning and helped me find my literary voice. Thank you for being honest, patient, understanding, corrective, and encouraging along this journey.

To Carolyn Edlund, founder of Artsy Shark and my business mentor, who took my creative ideas and guided my creative expression toward the writing of this book. I appreciate you knowing how to help me and when to consult others to support me along the journey.

To Steve Bennett, founder of AuthorBytes, whose creative mind was able to bring my words to life and who challenged me to be a better author, communicator, and consultant.

Additionally, I have been blessed to have a village of friends in my life who collectively represent over 200 years of friendship, and who have served as wise counsel, confidants, colleagues, sounding boards, laughing partners, travel companions, and protectors. My deepest thanks to you all: Dr. Kendra (China) DeWalt, Candace Ellerbe, LaToya R. Blaylock, Dr. Thea R.A. Shaw, Kelley S. Banks, Zeretha Brickhouse, Nicole Nelson, and Dr. A'Shawn L. Mitchell. You have been my strength when I was weak, my light when I could not see, my brains when I could not think, my stability when I was shaky, and my voice of reason during life's challenges. Thank you for your support and for all you have invested in me.

CONTENTS

INTRODUCTION

Believe it or not, but talking may in fact be the enemy of your ability to effectively communicate and connect with another person. On the surface, that statement may seem bizarre. But think about it like this: You've likely experienced relationships with friends or family members where something happened either to you or the other person, the dynamics of the relationship changed, and you didn't know what to do. You didn't know what to say. Talking about the situation (if you even tried to do that) didn't help. It actually made it worse! Over time, no one talked about the situation ... ever. It became a taboo topic. Unfortunately, when this happens, silence, guilt, shame, and even judgment creep into the relationship. This book is about how to stop merely talking and start communicating more effectively with those you care about when these taboo topics manifest, so you can maintain healthy, long-term relationships.

Full disclosure: I am a communication scientist. You may wonder what that is and what a communication scientist does. Well, I have a Doctor of Philosophy in communication studies, with a focus in health communication. That means I research theories, identify and apply practical ways about how people do and do not communicate, what topics folks are and are not willing to communicate about, what impacts the ability to communicate, and what we can do to improve our communication for understanding. I am particularly interested in what folks will and will not discuss with others as well as with health care providers about personal health, health behaviors, and disease. I am curious about why people will not discuss an illness or new onset of symptoms, even with medical professions. Equally, if they do, what makes them decide to share it and with whom? Yes, it is a science. Over the years, I've studied many areas of communication, including interpersonal conflict, various forms of stigma, doctor-patient communication, intercultural communication, family communication, persuasion, and disclosure, just to name a few. As you can see, communication science is a large field that is continually growing.

With all of that said, I am also a Black American woman born in Houston, TX (from the Northside). Do not let education, degrees, and credentials fool you. I am a professional, but I also understand how to take off my earrings in the street when necessary. I am a ride-or-die type of friend. I will stand ten toes down when everybody else is running away.

I take all the knowledge and scientific information I've learned and use my voice to make all the technical jargon applicable to your everyday life. If you cannot relate to the scenarios or figure out how to apply what you learn in this book to your life, then I have not completed my assignment. The words in these pages are not based on what I've heard or read but on what I have lived or what I have helped others live through. I am here to help you become the best version of yourself through communication.

You may be curious as to how I even found out about such a profession and what made me want to build a career in communication science. Well, the short answer is that it was a crooked road for me to get here. I did not follow a clear and straight path to becoming a communication scientist. My interest in better communication started because I felt communication had been stifled early in my life. Oftentimes in relationships, I felt that I was not given the whole story. I was expected, even required, to keep secrets within certain relationships. Taboo topics, or subjects never to be discussed, seemed to exist in many of the relationships early in my life. At a young age, I learned what not to talk about and which people not to talk to. My voice was muted. My opinion did not matter. My feelings were not taken into consideration. But I also understood that communication did matter. Not only did it matter, but most of us get it wrong. Most of us misunderstand each other because we communicate poorly.

As I grew into my womanhood, I was very clear that I had a voice, and I was going to use it. I would no longer allow others to mute me. Today, I say what I mean, and I mean what I say. Period. And anyone who knows me personally will tell you that I am straight forward. You will know exactly where you stand with me, and you will not be confused about my position when communicating with me. As a result, honesty is one of my core values. Communicating the truth is also one of my core values. I am very conscious of the words I use and of the words others use with me.

I have always been fascinated by the fact that communication is a requirement in life. Communication is all around us. You might say we even have communication overload. It comes at us from every angle: the television, social media, the phone, commercials, movies, neighbors, the news, billboards, friends, family, coworkers—the list is endless. So, if we have so many mediums of communication and we all must communicate constantly, how do so many of us, myself included, get it wrong at times? Why do we sometimes feel that we don't know what to communicate ... or that we need a "do over" for something we said and wish we could take back?

I find it interesting that a communication curriculum is not built into our educational system. We need English, math, and many other core classes to graduate high school, but communication is rarely required. Even more, we don't learn how communication impacts and affects daily life, our health, and relationships, and yet it does. Sure, you can take a communication course as an elective in college and you can choose communication as a major, but aside from that, there is no defined instruction nor training in primary school before you get to college. What if you don't go to college?

Because of this, most of us learn communication along the way. In reality, it's more like a hit or miss approach. We try something and if it works, we keep doing it. If it doesn't, we stop. Well, communication is so much more complex than that. And it is in the complexity where I enjoy helping people own their communication. Yes, own it.

With all that said, my experience in communication goes way beyond the academic and professional level. I have also written this book from personal experience as someone who has long-standing friendships with an average span of 20 years or more with each one of them. Over the years, our friendships have gone through changing seasons. Sometimes, we have been close and other times distant or out of touch all together. In time, we have found our way back to each other.

I also have family members whom I am estranged from and others I rarely speak with. While you cannot decide who you are related to, there is value in connecting and being in a relationship with people who share your lineage. Reflecting on family relationships provides the answer to some of the most pressing questions about who we are, why we do what we do, why we think the way we think, and the origin of our talents and natural abilities. Yes, family connections are important, but they can also be some of the most challenging to maintain. I admit that I have not always gotten it right. But I have found strategies you can use in your relationships with friends and family members to turn the tide on those difficult to discuss topics.

You Don't Say is based on both my professional and personal experiences. In this book, I share real-life examples of how people just like you react and respond in these challenging communication situations. In Part 1, you will get a better sense of why communication often breaks down. You will also learn strategies to help you shift from talking to communicating. In Part 2, you'll discover how to restart, restore, and reconnect relationships. You will learn that there are reasons why you are not communicating, and reasons why you have been unable to communicate despite wanting to so desperately. Maybe you've felt paralyzed by fear to even begin fixing the relationship, or perhaps you are questioning if the relationship can be fixed. I will help you through all these issues and more.

To get the most out of this book, I encourage you to do three things:

1. Read the book and understand the Relationship Reset model.
2. Filter your personal relationships through the framework provided.
3. Intentionally communicate so others engage with you, enabling you to address the taboo topic and restore the relationship.

As you begin reading this book, always remember that people change. Relationships change. Communication is the through line that drives that change. By using the strategies detailed in this book, you can be the driver of change in your relationships.

May you be blessed for instigating true communication in your personal relationships.

PART 1

UNRAVELING THE COMMUNICATION DILEMMA

CHAPTER 1

Why Relationships Go Bad

Let's face it ... maintaining strong relationships and communicating effectively with others is hard. Even though I am a communication scientist who helps healthcare organizations identify gaps in their health messaging, whether it is to patients, the greater community, or amongst themselves, I, too, get communication wrong sometimes. In fact, we all get communication wrong at some point—some of us more often than not. But why is something we do every day since toddlerhood so confusing? The challenge is that most people assume they know how to communicate. It's one of those things we take for granted. Unfortunately, even though we know how to talk, few of us have been taught proper communication skills. To make matters worse, it gets even more complicated when we are trying to communicate with close friends and family members.

Thanks to movies and perhaps even our own well-meaning family members and friends, we've been led to believe that communication is simple. But if it's so simple, how do so many of us get to a point in relationships where we don't know how to interact with a friend or family member anymore? What's even more interesting is that many of us can't explain how the relationship got to the point where we can be both present and absent at the same time when we are with a certain person. We know something changed in the relationship, something happened to one or both of us, but we won't talk about it with each other. The communication just doesn't happen. Even though we desperately want more for the relationship, we don't know how to make that "more" possible or what the "more" even is. Instead, we keep moving along in the relationship, feeling there are taboo topics that are off-limits and issues we no longer discuss. We feel the deterioration of the relationship and we silently yearn for things to go back to how they used to be ... or at least not to be what it is now.

The relationship deterioration often happens gradually. We have all been there, or at least we have seen others go through it. Best friends for over 20 years suddenly start hanging out less and less. The phone calls become less frequent. Before you know it, five years have passed, and they don't even know how to get in contact with each other anymore. Both are left wondering: How did we get to this point? What happened to the friendship? Why can't we get back to the friendship we used to have?

These kinds of problems don't just happen amongst friends; these issues bleed over into families too. For example, a family is very close. Spending every holiday together and getting together several times a month to play games or watch movies is standard. Over the years, the visits become less frequent. In time, no one gets together anymore. In fact, several family members stop talking to each other altogether. A few family members recall a fight about something, but nobody really knows what it was about. All they know is that the family isn't what it used to be. There's chatter between a few family members but nobody talks about what happened. Everyone is left wondering: How did we get here?

Here's another example: An uncle takes his nephew fishing every Saturday. One Saturday, he doesn't show up, and hasn't shown up since. The family doesn't bring up "Uncle Mike" anymore; they stopped talking about him completely. The nephew wonders why Uncle Mike is suddenly absent. "Where is he? Why doesn't he come around anymore? Why can't I talk about him? What did I do to make him stop coming to see me?"

Many of us find ourselves in these types of situations and don't know what to do about it. It seems that talking about the situation or taboo topic might work, but we don't know where to begin. How does that conversation start? If it did start, what would we say? It's like we are living a double life: a public life acting as if everything is fine and a private life where we are angry, disappointed, or tormenting ourselves by playing events over in our head, hoping to figure out exactly what happened, when it happened, and why it happened.

In my communications studies, I've learned that people's willingness to express their opinion is a function of how they perceive public opinion. Basically, people will be more confident and outspoken with their opinion when they notice that their opinion is shared among a group of people. However, if someone notices that their opinion is not accepted by the group, they are more likely to remain silent. At this point, you may be thinking that if we are talking about a taboo topic that exists between you and your mom, that is not a group. That is true. But it is also true that if there is an issue between you and your mom, chances are that other people, family, and friends of either you or your mother know about it. Not only do they know about it, but they now form "the group" that sets the standard of acceptance by which you are measured. The very existence of known and unknown groups who will either accept your opinions and beliefs or dismiss them further complicates the communication process.

Because we often don't know what to do or say in these situations, silence, at least about a particular subject, becomes part of the relationship. Rules are now a part of the relationship, yet nobody told us about them. Who made these rules? What are these rules? Where did these rules come from? How are we supposed to know these rules? Why are we expected to follow them? We are seemingly left with more questions than answers. As a result, we are left feeling sad, angry, confused, and sometimes lonely because we miss the relationship before "it" happened.

Tension is Real

Let's all agree that any relationship worth having is hard work. Relationships require an investment from us—to give when we don't have (piecing together bail money for a brother), to show up when we are tired (helping a friend move after a failed marriage), to listen when we don't have the time (coaching a friend through some job interview practice), and to understand that presence is more important than sending flowers (sitting in silence, rubbing the back of a friend who is burying a mother). It doesn't matter the nature of the relationship, navigating life and the experiences that come with being in a relationship with another person can be painfully difficult at times.

Just because we have friends doesn't mean we know how to build friendships. Just because we are around people who we are biologically related to does not mean we know how to be a family. Any relationship that has endured for any significant length of time has had to navigate through difficult and tough situations that affect how the people in the relationship interact with each other. That's what being in a relationship is all about. You weather the good times (purchase of a new home, the birth of a baby, a job promotion, starting a business) as well as the bad times (the addictions, the tragic murder of a loved one, the bankruptcy, the depression diagnosis, and living with chronic medical conditions).

However, life-altering moments can create change in a person and hover over the course of the relationship like a cloud, never disappearing, just following. When this happens, either one or both people don't know how to interact with the other person anymore. We have all experienced situations like this. For example, a dear friend is diagnosed with multiple sclerosis. The friend becomes withdrawn and is not as outgoing as they used to be. As a friend, you're not sure what to do. You rushed over when you first heard the news and stayed up all night crying with them. You offered to go out to your favorite restaurant, to have a movie night, and to go to medical appointments for support. Nothing seemed to help. But the friend is now secretive and private, nothing like they used to be before the diagnosis. You don't know what to say or do, but you do know you want your friend back. The connection has been fractured.

Or, how about the father recently released from prison? He doesn't know his adult daughter because he spent her entire childhood behind bars. And the daughter doesn't know her father. Neither knows what communication should look like for them.

These situations are real. These situations happen to all of us. These situations leave us feeling uncertain. Close friends become familiar strangers. That father just mentioned earlier? His daughter calls him by his first name because it's more fitting of how they interact with each other. When we are unsure, we typically remain in the current situation until something changes. We don't know what our role is. We don't know what we are allowed to do or say. That's when tension creeps in.

We call it tension because there is a physical or mental strain on the relationship. It creeps in without warning. Realistically, we feel heartbroken because we perceive a sense of loss or hopelessness of what will never be again. But we also feel our stomach turn into knots every time the person is around or even calls. We are worried about what will happen. Will there be an outburst or deafening silence when we meet up? We are angry about what has already happened and wonder why it occurred. We replay different scenarios in our head of what might be said or how we might respond. We may even just *ghost* the person because it's easier to walk away and vow never to make contact again than to deal with the feelings, emotions, and the unknown.

The Elephant in the Room

This tension exists because something happened that we consider *taboo*. What does taboo mean in the context of a relationship?

Here's an example: Suppose you have a friend who is having an extramarital affair. You believe it's wrong, but who are you to pass judgment? You were involved with a married person before, so you feel you have no room to share your opinion. But what do you do? Do you accept it? Do you tell the spouse about the affair? Do you avoid the spouse because you feel guilty for keeping a secret? Do you keep the secret? Do you go on double dates when asked to join? If you agree, are you complicit in the affair? How does this friendship work now? You feel lost about how to manage the new way the friendship works. There are so many questions with few answers.

The friendship has weathered through far worse times over the years but now seems different. Your friend expects you to welcome this "home wrecker" and go along with the whole thing. You wonder if your friend is having a midlife crisis. You have no one to discuss the situation with, and you want no part in it. When it blows up—and it will blow up—you don't want to be anywhere near the fallout. But you've been friends with this person for more than 20 years. So you show up, but not as often. You talk, but not as frequently. And you certainly don't talk about the affair.

What about the sister who is stuck in an abusive relationship? You want her to leave her partner, but she won't. Every time she talks about the "relationship," you find it's easier to remain silent because she doesn't want to make a change. It is painful watching her go through this, and you feel helpless. To feel useful or protective in some way, you pack an "escape" bag in case you have to get her out of the house in a hurry. She has no idea the bag is in the trunk. It's a painful secret that you have learned to live with. Unfortunately, it affects the relationship. You are quieter, not as talkative. You usually wait and see what she will say or do and respond to that because the abuse has become the center of how she makes decisions. Nothing about your relationship with her is the same. You decide to keep quiet about your feelings and the impact her situation is having on you. You simply don't talk about the abuse.

How about the friend with fertility issues? What do you do with that? What are you supposed to say when your friend calls and says, "We just had miscarriage number three"? The husband has a child from a previous relationship but would like a baby with his wife. The wife has never had any children and feels inferior as a woman for not being able to bring a baby into the world. How do you support both of your friends? Unfortunately, when this situation comes up between friends, most people avoid any topic that has anything to do with babies. They're careful not to bring up the topic of baby showers and scared to even share any pregnancy news. Others may say something they believe to be helpful, like "You can always try again." Or they ask if adoption has been explored as an option. Saying any of this is not helpful. Because the situation can be so awkward, you decide it is better to try to shield them from the pain by not asking them about fertility at all. Of course, that means there are now issues you don't talk about. It has become taboo.

What about the uncle who is a recovering alcoholic? Do you hide all the liquor when he comes around? You decide to never discuss anything that has to do with drinking. In fact, you didn't even show him pictures from your last vacation because you went to a tequila factory and didn't want to "make him feel weird." To make matters worse, your aunt mentioned that your uncle is "on edge" and is worried about him relapsing, so you remain quiet about the whole situation.

How about the grandfather who molested your brother and a cousin? The grandfather still comes over for family gatherings. Everyone knows what happened, yet no one has ever spoken about it out loud. Your brother and cousin are supposed to act as if everything is fine. There is a quiet expectation for everyone to act as if it did not happen for the sake of the family to "get along." Realistically no one is getting along, and everyone is either confused or angry that everyone acts as if nothing happened.

All these scenarios are real. We all face these types of situations at some point in a friendship and within our families. But when these situations occur, we feel strange and unsure of what to do or say. Usually, we say the wrong thing, or we say nothing, because we believe the issue to be taboo. We want to communicate about our feelings and the impact on the relationship, but we don't know how. More importantly, we have no idea how the other person will react. So, it's easier to stay silent.

As a result of this silence, these situations go unaddressed, are avoided, and are kept in secret, leading to great tension and strain within families and across friendships. The tension and strain can show up in many ways. You can have family members take sides. Some want to talk about the elephant in the room while others want to keep the secret, causing folks to go months or even years without speaking. Fights, both verbal and physical, can occur because of it. You can have friends stop talking as regularly as they used to. Soon, days turn to weeks, which turn to months. Before you know it, a few years have passed, and you just lost touch. You thought you would be best friends until the end, and now you don't talk to each other at all.

Some of us must decide who we are going to be friends with after a divorce is final. You don't want to choose, but you feel like you must because each person has demanded that you can't be friends with the other person. So, you befriend one and unfriend the other, and you don't talk about it.

This is how taboo topics are born in every relationship. Taboo topics create the tension between individuals in relationships and within families. The tension creates feelings of awkwardness, anxiety, confusions, heartache, and emotional instability. We may even feel physically sick, sweat profusely, get headaches, or cry. We experience a wide range of emotions when these situations happen in our lives and in our relationships. Since we are ill-equipped to communicate with others in these situations, we decide to not communicate at all.

Taboo Topics Exposed

Formally, the word "taboo" means "a ban or inhibition from social custom or aversion." While taboo is generally limited to offensive and inappropriate words, ethnic-racial-gender slurs, profanity, insults, etc., I extend the idea of taboo to more than words. Taboo words are born from situations, circumstances, and events. Taboo is something considered forbidden, because people generally think it is morally wrong. But who determines what is "morally wrong"? How are morals even defined? What are the morals based on? Whose morals are they?

For example, consider the taboo topic of abortion. In 1973, Roe v Wade was a landmark ruling from the US Supreme Court that established the constitutional right to an abortion. Forty-nine years later, on June 24, 2022, the Supreme Court, in a 5-4 decision, overturned Roe v. Wade. Unfortunately, and sadly, this is a very present example of how one group can impose their morals on another, or in this case on an entire nation.

Before the decision and in its aftermath, particularly now that abortion is illegal in some states, there has been cultural and social discord around the mere mention of the word. Why? The short answer is because there are opposing beliefs about what is the "right" decision. Some people believe a woman has the right to decide what to do with her body. Others argue that the fetus must be protected at all costs. Some have argued that abortion should be allowed only in the case of rape or incest, or if the mother's life is in danger, while others think those factors have no bearing and the woman must still carry the fetus to term. Some believe the father has rights to the fetus. In fact, countless opinions exist about abortion. As such, I think we can all agree that in most circles abortion is considered taboo. Because there is a longstanding and painful history around abortion, both culturally and personally, most people do not want to talk about it or express their opinion in public. (Although since Roe v Wade was overturned, we are seeing the topic of abortion garner a greater voice, and folks are emboldened to defend and share their opinions more openly.)

Practically speaking, a taboo topic is anything that carries some degree of secrecy if there is a belief that the mere mention would garner controversy, incite division, stigmatize certain people or groups, or instigate drama due to the perceived "badness" of the behavior, for whatever reason, by an individual. This itself creates problems in the relationship because issues are identified as taboo based on judgments made by an individual, which then informs decisions, which ultimately lead to actions that affect the relationship.

Here is how that happens. Let's consider two people with two different abortion experiences. One person has an abortion, and another pays for their girlfriend to get an abortion. These two scenarios can play out very differently but have similar communicative outcomes. Let's first consider the person who has the abortion. For her, it was a difficult choice to make, but she believes it to be the right choice. She comes from a religious family and believes that abortion is a sin. She knows it goes against all she believes in. But she also knows she can't possibly take care of a child right now. She is barely out of childhood herself. Even more, the man who impregnated her can barely take care of himself. The relationship was really a one-night stand that lasted way too long. The only thought that comes to her mind is: "I can't have this baby right now with this guy. My life will be forever changed if I have this baby."

A friend offers to drive her to the abortion clinic and stay through the weekend to ensure there are no complications and to keep her company. The friend believes getting the abortion is wrong, murder even. Her thoughts turn to judgment rather quickly. "How can she do this? How can she kill her baby? How did I become friends with someone who could do this?"

The one getting the abortion is grieving for a baby that will never make it into the world. She is also uncertain of how her friend and others will judge her decision. Thoughts are running through her head: "Will I ever be able to get pregnant again? Have I caused irreversible damage to my body? Do I deserve to have a baby after this? What if I can't get pregnant again? Am I going to hell?"

Due to the self-shame and fear of judgment, silence is the communicative choice. The friend is also unsure what to do or say afterward. The friend finds it difficult to hide her feelings. To her, abortion is wrong … period. But they have a 10+ year friendship that can't just go away because of this.

Neither one of them knows how to reconcile how they feel with what has happened. Both have made judgments, about themselves and the other person. They both decide that not talking about it is the best thing to do for the friendship. In fact, the two never discuss the abortion again. It has become a taboo topic, and because of this unaddressed issue festering below the surface, their relationship is never as close as it used to be.

Now, let's consider the person who pays for their romantic partner to get an abortion. It all started when the phone call came, "I'm pregnant." His first thoughts were, "Is it mine? How far along is she? I wore a condom. I don't want to have a baby right now and I don't want to have a baby with her." So, he calls a friend:

"Yo, she's pregnant! What am I going to do?"

Friend: "Did you ask her what she wants to do?"

"You know I can't ask her that."

Friend: "Why not?"

"Because you know how women feel about all that."

Friend: "Bruh, if you don't want to be owned for the next 18 years, you better figure out how to ask her what she is going to do. Plus, you know that price goes up the further along she is."

"Right, right."

Friend: "You know what you have to do."

She gets the abortion. He's not sure how to feel about it because he wasn't sure if it was the right thing to do. But his friend was really pushing for the abortion. He feels torn because part of him is sad that he will never meet his first child. He is mad at himself for listening to his friend and for encouraging her to get the abortion. After the abortion, he calls his friend less and less often. He's unsure how to hang out like they used to because the friend may ask about the girl and how she's doing. The truth is, he wants his friend to ask how *he* is doing. He knows his friend has paid for several girls to have abortions over the years, but this is all new to him and hasn't been easy. He has started having nightmares about it. He wonders what he'll say to his future wife. Should he ever tell her that he paid for an abortion? He thinks he can't tell his friend everything he is feeling because he doesn't want to look weak or soft. So he keeps silent about the abortion and doesn't mention it again. Just as in the previous example, a taboo topic has infiltrated the relationship and caused it to splinter.

These are very different situations centered on the same taboo topic, and both arrived at similar communicative outcomes: silence. Because of unspoken judgments, both people made the decision to not speak about the abortion. When judgements and feelings of shame become part of the relationship, communication suffers. Regardless of what the judgment is about, or how the decision is rationalized, or even what actions play out, it is unmistakable that a change in the relationship occurred, and neither person knows how it happened.

The Unspoken Rule

By design, most people do not communicate about taboo topics nor do they do anything to resolve the tension because it is an unspoken rule not to. How does all this start in the first place?

We learn communicative behaviors. We learn them from our families ("Don't talk about your cousin's time in prison"). We learn them from culture ("Don't put my business in the street."). We learn them from society ("It's impolite to ask someone [suspected of being an immigrant] where they are from"). We learn them from friends ("We don't talk about the molestation"). We learn them at school and at work ("Don't ask anyone how much money they make"). Just because we learned these behaviors from outside influences does not mean we have to accept them and adopt them as the way we communicate. We can take responsibility for our role in a relationship and be intentional about how we communicate. We can choose to communicate about the taboo areas within our relationships that are creating tension, which is how you dissolve the tension.

We just discussed a few issues that many people consider taboo and typically hold in secret or shame. What is interesting is that not everyone considers the same issues to be taboo. Everyone has a personal position about what is and is not taboo. Though the word taboo is clearly defined in a dictionary, it is a very subjective term. Subjectivity allows everyone to view the world through their personal interpretation, biases, prejudices, and preconceived ideas—not necessarily facts.

Unfortunately, this subjectivity is the reality in which people live, make decisions, communicate, and function in relationships regardless of whether it aligns with fact or not. This creates an even bigger problem. We never really know what another person considers taboo until it occurs. And even then, we may not be aware the person considers the situation taboo because we don't discuss taboo topics! But we will know when something considered taboo has happened because there is awkwardness, estrangement, uncomfortableness, shame, guilt, and secrets when there wasn't any of that before. Even more frustrating is that because we rarely discuss taboo topics, there is an inherent and unspoken understanding to not speak about it—ever. This leads to another problem. Having a taboo topic fester within a relationship is like a malignancy. It steadily and quietly grows without causing pain … until it does. And when it does, it is usually catastrophic to the relationship (you have a big argument that results in you not speaking again) and catastrophic to the people in the relationship (you have a sense of loss and sadness). It can even bleed onto others close to the people in the relationship, as when a grandmother tries to reconcile an estranged mother and son and is criticized by both sides and now doesn't talk to either of them.

Failed Attempts to Resolve the Tension

When people sense tension in a relationship that wasn't present before, they attempt to resolve the tension by "talking about it." Unfortunately, when we talk about it, we often say and do the wrong things. Period. We just do. Why? Because we learned communicative behaviors and skills from outside influences. We never leaned into our true and authentic selves and communicated about what we wanted and needed in relationships. We want to relieve the tension to make the relationship tolerable, but we fail and sometimes make it worse.

We may try one or more of the following five ways to resolve tension communicatively in a relationship. Though what follows is not an exhaustive list of strategies, I have highlighted the most common ones that you will likely know. None of these are effective, and they often lead to greater tension in the relationship. They are passive aggression, comedy/sarcasm, explosive outbursts, ignore, and stage an intervention. Let's look at each in detail.

1. Passive aggression is a deliberate and masked way of expressing covert feelings of anger. It involves a range of behaviors designed to get back at another person without acknowledging the underlying anger. Plainly, it is unresolved hostility. And it can be cyclical. We all

know people who do this. We may even do this. It does not work yet it is a go-to option for many of us.

You may use passive aggression as an attempt to resolve tension because there is an inherent belief that people will respond the way you want when you direct mean acts or words toward them. The belief is that if the other person feels enough pain, they will change. You may even assume the other person will eventually decode the messages you are sending because "who would not pick up on the messages?" However, according to Pastor Rick Warren, author of *Purpose Driven Life* and pastor of Saddleback Church, people do not change when they see the light; people change when they feel the heat. I agree with his sentiment. This is to say that people do not change because they have new information or they become aware of certain truths. People do not turn from risky behavior because they get caught, get shot, "hit rock bottom," or even end up in prison. The fact is that people change when they feel there is no other option. When people finally face themselves and live in the consequences of what they have done, who they have become, and who they are in that moment, and they cannot run or hide from that reflection anymore, only then *might* they change. Despite that truth, we mistakenly believe that somehow another person will "pick up on a subliminal message." That's simply not how people are wired.

For example, let's consider drug addiction. A close friend has smoked marijuana all their life—no big deal. Right? After years of marijuana use, they slowly start acting differently. They don't show up when you plan to meet up at happy hour. They start calling in sick to work. They also seem to go missing for days at a time. As a friend, you suspect more is going on than just marijuana use, but you aren't sure. You go to visit and find some sketchy and suspicious people that are referred to as "new friends." You notice a crack pipe and needles on the coffee table. In complete disbelief, you storm out of the house. But before you do, you say, "I know you smoked weed, but I thought you were smart enough to stay away from the hard drugs!" To add insult to injury, you later drive over to the friend's house to leave narcotics anonymous pamphlets in the mailbox.

Therein lies the problem. What is the message? What exactly should your friend realize from these antics? And even more, what action are they supposed to take after being subjected to judgment, shaming, and overall meanness?

If you do not communicate your authentic self, nothing will work. In this case, you want to tell your friend that watching them physically deteriorate due to drug use is heartbreaking. You want to tell them that you avoid spending time with their kids because you don't want to explain addiction. You want to tell them that you are angry that you lost a best friend and don't know if you will get them back. You want to tell them that your life has changed too because of this addiction. But instead, you just leave pamphlets in a mailbox.

2. Comedy or the use of sarcasm expresses hostility aloud, but in socially acceptable, indirect ways. There is always a bit of truth in comedic quips—that's what makes it funny and sometimes painful. People have used comedy to mask pain for centuries. Think about Kevin Hart's breakthrough comedy special *Laugh at my Pain,* or Chris Rock's classic *Bring the Pain* comedy tour. In each of these, they use comedy to talk about real-life problems, often taboo topics that are not talked about like drug addiction and imprisonment, which can be funny because we all have experienced the deafening silence these subjects can bring in a friendship or within a family. Communication through humor is an important way to make stories more memorable, characters more compelling, and causes more accessible.

On the flip side, people can use comedy as a tool to express frustration in a subtle and acceptable way. We often revert to comedy as an attempt to resolve tension because we believe that it's best to deliver a negative message while everyone is laughing and having fun. We mistakenly think that if someone is laughing, they are more open and receptive to what is being said and will "take the hint."

Let's revisit the drug addiction example. After the unsuccessful efforts of passive aggression, you think comedic outbursts may work. Your friend was able to get together enough to come to a backyard BBQ at your house. While music plays and folks dance in the yard, a few of you are sitting around the table eating and talking. The conversation turns to the recent burglaries in the area. Several friends mention extra precautions they are taking to avoid being burglarized, while others make jokes about different types of alarm systems and the idea of getting a dog for protection. Then you say, "You don't have to worry about buying alarms and getting dogs when your best friend will steal $20 off your dining table." An awkward silence descends on the group, but then is quickly followed by hysterical laughter and high-fives. Clearly upset, your friend walks off in shame. The others don't know that this really happened—that your best friend has stolen money from you to buy drugs.

Instead of chasing after your friend to offer solace or at least attempt to talk about it, you shake your head in disbelief. You thought they might have $20 on them to pay you back and offer an apology. But because they walked off, you think they are mad because you "told everybody" what they did. But you'll never know because you never talk about it.

3. Explosive outbursts are actions and/or responses that are disproportionate to the situation at hand (e.g., impulsive shouting, screaming, or excessive reprimanding triggered by relatively inconsequential events). Outbursts can be physical or verbal. Everyone gets angry at times. Anger can range from a slight irritation to full-blown rage in a split second. Often, we try to bottle up or control our emotions, until we can't hold it in any longer. We then resort to verbal outbursts because it feels good to let it all out. It releases pressure to yell and scream at someone or to jump on somebody and fight them. It gives you control over your actions, and nobody can do anything about it. All that matters is you were able to get your point across for everyone to understand. Unfortunately, outbursts seem to come out of nowhere, and typically the people who are the intended target or innocent bystanders are left confused. Oftentimes, they are left wondering, "Where did that come from?" or "What caused that?"

If we keep with the drug addiction analogy, we can see how outbursts happen but are not helpful. In this case, your friend has further spiraled down the addiction hole and has been kicked out of their house. They are now living at either homeless shelters or on the couches of family members who feel sorry for them. You get a phone call from your friend asking if you can come and pick them up. They are stranded on the other side of the city. They explain that some guys beat them up and stole their car. Frustrated, you yell into the phone, "You deserve everything you get. You ruined your life. Drugs cost you, your family, and most of your friends. I don't know why you even called me. I won't help you anymore. I'm sick of playing clean-up for your mistakes. You did this to yourself. Nobody made you use drugs. Nobody forced a pipe in your mouth or a needle in your arm. I don't know who you are anymore. I am sick of this!" To emphasize your point, you hang up the phone without waiting for a response.

Unfortunately, the outburst has only delivered more harm. The friend made the phone call because they thought you were the only friend they had left. They know that drugs have ruined their life. In fact, your friend wishes they never started any of it. But they can't stop now—they are a drug addict and don't know how to stop. Your outburst arose from anger because you love your friend and can't stand to see them spiral out of control. You hope that maybe hearing "the truth" will set them straight once and for all. You are both left with feelings of pain and a sense of loss, as well as the lingering thoughts of how to get the friendship back. But you'll never know because you never talk about it.

4. Ignore (act as if nothing happened) is impossible to do, but many try. Even if we're not thinking about it and not doing anything about it, we still know about the problem subconsciously. The fact that we are choosing to ignore it creates space for unresolved emotions to manifest in other parts of the relationship. The act of ignoring can manifest in several ways – we can stop talking altogether ("I will not call them ever again"), we can walk away when the subject is brought up ("I left something in my car"), we can claim ignorance about the subject completely ("No, I didn't know that"). Though not an exhaustive list, these are common options most people choose.

As it relates to drug addiction, in today's society, it is unfortunately acceptable to ignore the problem. For example, one day as you're walking down the street to the local coffee shop, you see your drug addict friend sitting on the corner. You choose to busy yourself on your phone and not make eye contact. You hope your friend doesn't notice you. But you're not the only person who ignores them now. They tried to show up at their son's baseball game, but the coach had security escort them off the field at the urging of their ex-partner. Even their own mother ignores the problem. She was visiting with family, and someone asked how her kids were doing. She interrupted the question and excused herself to go to the bathroom. Sometimes, it's easier to ignore the person and the issue than it is to communicate about it directly.

5. Intervention is commonly associated with addiction to motivate people to seek treatment. However, we can use interventions to address a myriad of destructive behaviors (e.g., adultery, failure to take care of responsibilities) that are affecting individuals and those around them in a negative way. Usually, we try intervention as the last option, the last hope people have of making a change.

An intervention makes demands and demonstrates a united front. The goal is to show a person that family and friends still love and care for them. But the only way it works is if everyone is allowed the opportunity to share earnest feelings about how the situation has impacted their life. An intervention is not about agreement or getting the facts straight; rather, it is about having a space and the opportunity to share feelings and emotions, not judgments. However, it is important to realize that just because those who participate in the intervention have hope of a perfect ending (the person will enter rehab) they must be willing to accept that the outcome may be unpredictable and could be nothing like what they imagined.

If we consider our drug addiction story one final time for an example of intervention, we learn that not everyone is receptive to the help that is being offered or to the love family and friends show as part of the process. In this case, you decide that you want to try and save your friend's life. You heard that they had a few stints in jail and are homeless now. All their family members have walked away because your friend has stolen from them or lied to them. Their family fears they can't help anymore. You reach out to your friend's ex-partner, mother, and a few cousins to join you in the intervention. Everyone agrees to participate but not before sharing their horror stories of what this person has done to them.

The day of the intervention finally arrives. You have a united front, and you all think this might work. Your friend shows up. Every person shares their feelings about how drug use has affected their lives: The loss of security whenever they come around ... the sadness of not having a child, cousin, or friend in their life anymore ... the embarrassment of seeing them panhandling on the streets. You all want this person to seek help.

Unfortunately, your friend thinks they have hurt too many people, caused too much damage, and will never get their life back on track. Your friend stands up and offers a heartfelt apology, "I am sorry for all the pain I have caused each of you." Then they storm out of the room. Everyone is shocked. You wonder, "What do we do now?" No one has an answer for what is next. It's too painful to talk about, so you never discuss it again.

Forging a Way Forward

All the ways we just discussed are typically how people attempt to resolve tension in a relationship. Because we feel we have no control, we try to gain control by talking about it—facing it head on. But this only adds additional stress and strain to the tension that already exists in the relationship. It leads to denying feelings of anger, leaves action open for interpretation, and creates an emotional roller coaster for everyone involved.

We can all agree that we do most of these things because we desperately want to get back to the place where the relationship was before the incident, but we don't know how. That doesn't mean we can't. It simply means that we must establish a new normal, new boundaries, and new expectations for the relationship. A new (and better) relationship is possible!

To transition to the new relationship, you must reconnect and re-establish the relationship by communicating about the tension. The work entailed to do so will not happen overnight. The path to the new relationship can be long and winding. The journey will be different for everyone and for every relationship. This work will require each person to take responsibility for their role and actions in the relationship. You can no longer wait and see what will happen. The time for action is now!

You will have to be deliberate and purposeful about your intentions, your actions, and your words. Others may not be receptive to what you are doing or saying. You may discover that the other person does not want a relationship. Maybe the other person doesn't want to communicate. That's okay. Because you are forging forward with the goal of understanding communication and being a more effective communicator, you will need to embrace a mindset shift. Ultimately, if you change your words and your mindset, you really can change your life and relationships. What you say, how you say it, and when you say it matters.

Your words hold immense power. Life and death are in the tongue. Death is not just physical. Emotional and mental death ("I am worthless. They only pretend to like me. I am damaged goods.") can come from the tongue, even if self-directed.

Words matter. YOUR words matter! Understanding communication matters, because true communication only occurs when there is understanding between people. That's why we are going to spend the next several chapters discussing interpersonal communication and how it greatly impacts life and relationships, as well as sharing tools and techniques that can get your relationships back on track.

Are you ready to resolve the tension in your relationships? Let's get going.

CHAPTER 2

Cultivate a Communication Mindset

If you want to interact comfortably with the other person again, you need to embrace the idea of a Relationship Reset. What is a Relationship Reset? It's an opportunity to begin the relationship anew, and it is necessary in order to alleviate the tension within the relationship. Most of us have long memories of events that are traumatic and painful to us, particularly those involving a close friend or family member, so it is unreasonable to believe that a Relationship Reset suggests we forget all the past years of the relationship. Quite the contrary! The past years and experiences in a relationship are actually an advantage you can use as a catalyst for change. In other words, to move forward in a relationship, you must first revisit the past times, the past pains, and past feelings you've intentionally not discussed in order to establish a new relationship. Yes, you want a new normal. But a *new normal* doesn't imply the old relationship and the past feelings, good or bad, are forgotten. Rather, it signifies the need to establish a new way in which you interact with the other person.

The starting point for a Relationship Reset is with each of us, individually, developing a communication mindset. No matter what type of relationship you're struggling with, whether with a parent, spouse, sister, friend, etc., communicating within that relationship is an individual responsibility. If the other person does not understand your intended idea or feeling, you have the responsibility to intentionally communicate for understanding. In other words, you need to ensure that the meaning of what you say is received as intended. Therefore, your first step is to strive to develop a communication mindset. That means thinking about the thoughts or beliefs that drive your mental attitudes and that predetermine your interpretations and responses to how you communicate with another in response to events, circumstances, and situations around you. Adopting this communication mindset requires a mental shift, because most people do not innately think this way. We all have to form the habit of having a communication mindset.

Like most habits, developing the habit of a communication mindset requires us to make certain decisions that support the new habit. In this case, we need to be aware that we are only responsible for what we do, not anybody else. I have been a student of famed psychologist Gary Chapman, author of *The Five Love Languages* and many other bestsellers, for years. He asserts that you cannot make anybody do anything. I wholeheartedly agree with him, both on a professional and personal level. As such, I apply the same message here that I believe bears repeating: you cannot make anybody do anything. Period. You are not responsible for how another person reacts to what you say. However, you are responsible for expressing yourself authentically and honestly in personal relationships. If you feel tension in a certain relationship, you need to resolve it for your own sake. Having a communication mindset is just as much about the work you are doing on yourself as it is about the relationship with the other person. It is really about understanding yourself and making peace with what has happened to you, with situations you intentionally or unintentionally caused, and with events that have affected you in some way. Then it's about harnessing the power in that understanding to communicate your raw feelings with someone close to you. This newfound sense of self-awareness gives you the strength and confidence needed to communicate any topic, because genuine communication requires audacity with humility.

Before we go any further, let's acknowledge that developing any new habit can be difficult. What we are doing now is no different. Developing a communication mindset requires you to move beyond what is comfortable. You must become comfortable with the uncomfortable. Why? Because comfort doesn't require any struggle or growth. Comfort is the status quo. Often, communication patterns become so comfortable that we fail to change or want to change how we interact with others.

What does that mean? Typically, we follow a script when we are communicating with others, especially those who are close to us, because we are operating from a space of history and past encounters. We all do this. For example, when a friend asks, "When are ya'll going to start having some kids?" Your response is, "When we get good and ready." This then becomes the script for this subject between the two of you for years to come.

These automatic, almost robotic, responses prohibit us from forging a new path because we default to what we usually say to each other. Our communication with each other becomes ineffective, predictable, and stale, which can create a divide over time. However, when you embrace a communication mindset, you are finally able to rewrite the old, ineffective script.

Talking vs. Communication

Though communication is a science, that does not mean the skills necessary to engage with another person effectively are so complicated that we cannot apply them in our daily life. For example, "talking" is a concept we all know and understand. In its simplest form, talking is the exchange of thoughts or opinions in spoken or sign language. Comparatively, "communication" is the successful conveying (understanding) or sharing of ideas and feelings. Most of us use the two terms interchangeably. And therein lies part of the problem. One of the greatest errors we make is the assumption that talking and communicating are created equal. Further, our belief that we are doing either one or both effectively inhibits us from pursuing change.

It is natural for us to talk with someone. It seems easy enough, right? Consider this example: You have a friend who seems to run hot and cold for no apparent reason. At some points, you two are very tight, and at other times your friend seems distant and aloof. You're not sure why the friend seems to see-saw with their personality, and you have never brought it up. One day you call your friend on the phone and the conversation goes something like this:

"Hey, what are you doing?"

Friend: "Nothing. I'm about to head over to the mall and see if I can find a shirt to go with these pants I have to wear tonight for this get-together."

"What mall are you going to?"

Friend: "Over to The Galleria."

"Oh? You trying to get that expensive drip?"

Friend: "Nah, it's just closer to where I am right now. It's a faster drive."

"Oh, alright. What time is your get-together?"

Friend: "From about 6-9."

"You want to hang out after?"

Friend: "Not tonight. I am really tired and plan to head home and just go to bed after."

"Alright. Holla at you later."

Friend: "Okay, bye."

This is a common conversation the two of you have during times when the relationship seems cold. It's factual with no intimate details or common friend chatter. The conversation is certainly simple enough on the surface. However, when we delve into the details, the difference between talking and communicating will become apparent.

- Let's consider the idea of the get-together. Each of us has a different perception of what a get-together is. In this context, your friend's idea of a get-together means meeting a few co-workers at a happy hour. Your idea of a get-together is the friend going to someone's house with a couple of people, very casual.

- Next, let's review the idea of the mall. Depending on your experiences, the mall can mean so many different things. The friend who is going to the mall considers The Galleria just like any other mall. To provide perspective, The

Galleria is Texas's largest shopping center and receives more than 30 million visitors a year. It has over 400 retail stores, more than 60 dining options, 13,000 parking spaces, and seven parking garages. Most people don't consider it "just like any other mall." In this example, let's say that your idea of a mall is something that offers about 100 stores and has a food court with about ten restaurants. Notice the difference?

- Now, let's unpack the idea of "going home to go to bed." You might think your friend is tired and had a long week, and maybe that's why they're so distant right now. You know how much they work so it makes sense they would be tired. Unfortunately, the truth is that your friend hasn't been getting much sleep, but not because they are tired from overworking. The friend is having those dreams again. They call them the "creepy molester dreams." The friend was molested as a kid for several years, and as an adult they experience times when the dreams come back. They're not really dreams, more like nightmares that replay over and over, highlighting different scenes and different days from the violations. The voice, the smell, the touch, the time of day … all of it comes to mind. So for the friend, there are times when it's more comfortable to stay up all night because the thought of sleeping is too frightening.

In this instance, we can see how easy it is to mistake talking for communicating. Two people are having two different conversations with each other at the same time, without even knowing it. You were simply checking in on a friend who seemed distant lately. But your friend was mentally processing the sleepless nights in the very moment and decided it was easier to say, "I'm going home and going to bed." Without saying a word, two people had a false sense of understanding one another, of communicating with one another, when they were really just talking. They totally missed each other.

How can people who have been friends for over 10 years have this kind of encounter? We can all understand how molestation is not a subject considered small talk; however, when we consider close relationships and friendships, we think we would know something like this has happened to a loved one. Sometimes, when we do learn about such a tragic event that has happened to someone we love, we may get upset that the information wasn't shared with us. We believe that "we should have known" and "should have been told." We may even believe that the person is keeping secrets.

Think about some of your recent conversations with friends and family.

- Were you just talking with the other person? Or were you truly communicating?
- What perceptions did you bring to the conversation?
- What previous experiences or encounters did you have with the person that affected the moment?
- Were you aware of the place from where your words, emotions, and reactions came from?

While we don't often acknowledge our past experiences with another person while we are in communication moments with them, we must do so to begin cultivating a communication mindset. When we fail to allow ourselves to be present with the feelings and emotions experienced in the context of a relationship with another person, we are hindering our ability to have authentic relationships with another. Ultimately, we are failing ourselves and the relationship.

Even worse, when there is tension in a relationship, it's common for the same communication scenario to play out repeatedly, simply because we don't know how to truly communicate. Instead, we think we have communicated. As George Bernard Shaw said, "The single biggest problem in communication is the illusion that it has taken place." Essentially, we all think we have communicated our point, but the other person has not received or understood the message. We think we are communicating, but we are really just talking. To think that we are doing something does not necessarily mean we are doing it.

Disclosing parts of our lives, cultures, and lived experiences to others is essential for real communication to take place. When we don't communicate, we make inferences, which leads to judgments. So, the real issue isn't the people or even the circumstances we find ourselves in. The real issue is that we encounter awkward situations and fail to gain common understanding, which results in us making judgments and creating our own reasons for why things are the way they are. What's the solution? Communicating with the other person!

The Mindset Shift

You now have the opportunity to move beyond thinking that you are communicating ... to intentionally seeking to be a better communicator. And it all starts with developing a communication mindset. In fact, once you embrace the idea of a communication mindset and begin to apply the power of it, you will be able to walk in your truth and instigate a Relationship Reset. To begin the mental shift, I offer three points as a guide:

1. Be aware of your perceptions
2. Ask questions
3. Repeat what you heard

Let's look at each point in detail.

1. Be aware of your perceptions:

Most of us don't have a true understanding of what other people's words really mean. We think we do, but we typically don't confirm their meaning of the words they used so that we have mutual understanding. We think that because we are speaking the same language, are from similar cultures, have shared interests, are related or have been friends for many years, that we understand each other. In some cases, that may be true. However, more often than we realize, we don't really understand. Being aware of perceptions means that we grasp the meaning *and* intent of what is said.

We can see this play out in the real-life example of a dinner party. If you were invited to a dinner party, what would you expect? When we receive an invitation to a dinner party, we don't usually think much about its meaning, because the general perception is that everyone has the same definition of a dinner party. So let's say you get invited to one. You dress nicely in a cute party dress or business casual outfit and pick up a moderately-priced bottle of wine. You expect about 5-10 people to attend, primarily couples. And you anticipate spending about 3-4 hours at the host's home, maybe longer if you all start a card game or watch a movie.

All of us rely on our past experiences to dictate our actions. We assume that a dinner party requires us to bring something for the host. We think this because we are using our perceptions (from TV, cultural norms, etc.) and personally lived experiences to define things, which can leave us having two different conversations in the same moment. So, before you respond yes or no to the dinner party invitation based on assumptions, it's imperative to ensure understanding. You do that with the next step.

2. Ask questions:

To ensure understanding, you have to ask a lot of questions. You may believe that most folks get annoyed when they are asked a series of questions. And if you are just rambling off a bunch of random questions that don't pertain to the situation, that may be true. However, when people understand why you are asking the questions, they are more amenable to the request. If you are genuinely curious and seeking answers to connect and communicate, then asking questions creates a safe space for sharing.

Let's go back to the dinner party example. Some questions you can ask are:

- "About how many people are you expecting?"
- "What wine or other drinks can I bring to compliment the dinner?"
- "About what time should we arrive?"
- "Should I bring a dish to share?"

These are the types of questions that can help you gain clear understanding.

You may feel like you are asking a lot of questions in the moment. In fact, you may think all the questions aren't necessary. You may feel some discomfort or embarrassment in the question asking process. But here's the truth: those are self-inflicted thoughts based on individual perception. You have no proof that anyone else thinks any of those things. Just because you think it, does not make it true. There is great value in asking questions so that you don't move through relationships thinking one thing, when in fact the other person is defining something completely different.

If you don't ask questions, you can experience surprises. Often, the surprises aren't fun. In our dinner party example, here's what could very well happen if you don't ask questions and instead just head over to the dinner party based on your past experiences and perceptions. You arrive at the host's home, and you learn they are grilling hamburgers and hot dogs in the backyard. Additionally, you discover that no one else is coming. It will be just two couples: the hosts and you and your plus one. They are drinking beer. They don't even like wine. You're there in your nice business casual clothes or party dress with your $80 bottle of wine. But your friends are dressed in shorts and T-shirts. You feel overdressed and a bit embarrassed that you interpreted the dinner party differently. In fact, you're actually a little mad at your friend for calling it a dinner party when in your mind it's "just a cookout."

By asking a few simple clarifying questions, you could have avoided this miscommunication and hurt feelings. So while asking questions may seem confrontational, it's really not. Natural curiosity that is purposed to understand the intent of someone's message should not be regarded as confrontational. It is about conveying an idea, thought, or feeling and then understanding another person's meaning and intentions. When you ask questions, you're making an attempt to gain common understanding. And when that happens, it makes all the difference.

But asking the questions and getting the answers is only part of the solution. Next you need to repeat what you heard—not the words the other person said, but what you heard. There's a big difference between the two, as we'll see in the next point.

3. Repeat what you heard:

After asking questions and receiving answers, you will want to repeat what was said in "your language" back to the person so they understand how you processed the words. Most people "hear" something completely different from the actual words that are spoken, yet we rarely know this because we don't repeat our interpretation of the words back to the person.

Repeating what you hear is critical because what was said and how you interpret what you hear are often very different things. Ideas and concepts can get lost in translation. In our dinner party example, if you had asked questions, you may have heard that dinner will be hamburgers and hot dogs. You may have then said back to your friend, "Oh? So this is a very low-key dinner," or "This is more like a cookout." None of those words came out of your friend's mouth; however, that is what you heard.

You may think it's strange or weird that they define a dinner party in this way. In fact, you might even form opinions about them based on this one instance. Unfortunately, we all easily form opinions about situations or people who do things or define things differently than we do. However, being aware of your perceptions, asking questions, and repeating what you heard can make all the difference in your relationships. In our dinner party example, when your friend was born, their mother died during childbirth. They didn't know their father; he wasn't even named on the birth certificate. As a result, your friend grew up in foster care. Though they managed to graduate high school, they never learned life skills. Learning how to cook, clean, wash clothes, manage money, and most other skills took a back seat to just trying to survive. While they lived in the group home, their few belongings often got stolen. They had to fight to get a bed or even eat a meal. They invited you over because they consider you a dear friend. For your friend, cooking dinner, even if it is hot dogs and hamburgers, is an expression of gratitude. In fact, that is a nice dinner in their house because they are barely making ends meet now, although they hide it well. But of course, none of this is shared or spoken out loud. Simply put, we just don't communicate very well.

Be Aware of Your Inferences

As noted earlier, perceptions and inferences shape our reality. The founding principle of communication science is that "one cannot *not* communicate," which implies that humans are continuously communicating. Even being silent is a way of communicating some kind of message. So it's impossible not to communicate. Non-communication doesn't exist. Even when we do nothing, verbally or nonverbally, we are transmitting something. The idea of continuously communicating may seem unbelievable or at the very least impossible. However, as soon as we perceive another person and share information—either verbally or physically—we are communicating. With that in mind, it is reasonable to accept the notion that communication can be intentional and unintentional, on purpose and accidental, and done consciously and unconsciously by all of us.

Though we communicate without knowing what we are communicating and to whom, it still affects how we interpret what we see and the way we interact with another person. We can apply this idea to a simple situation we have all experienced before: shopping at the grocery store. Let's imagine you enter the grocery store on a Saturday afternoon. A diverse crowd of people surrounds you. You see a child wearing pajamas and a cape, running away from their parents, and hitting every basket as they run away. You think, "That child has no discipline. Those parents didn't even dress their kid today. That child is going to get hurt." You keep walking through the store and head over to the produce department. You see an elderly lady with a younger woman who appears to be her daughter. You think, "How nice that she brought her mom to the grocery store. They look like they have a great relationship. I wish I had that kind of relationship with my mom." Next, you walk down the candy aisle. You notice a considerably overweight person standing in front of the chocolate candies. You immediately think, "The last thing they need is candy. How could you let yourself get that big in the first place? Just call Dr. Nowzaradan (Dr. Now) from *My 600-lb Life* and do the work to lose the weight!" You finally make it to the checkout line, pay for your groceries, and head to the car to go home. You didn't know or speak to any of the people you saw in the grocery store, but you quickly made-up stories about them and took those fictional stories as truth. Isn't it funny that this is how we think and interpret information we see?

In this example, we can see that communication occurs naturally, without even thinking about it, even when running a simple errand like going to the grocery store. We are simultaneously communicating about ourselves and making inferences about those around us. Inferences, which are guesses we make or opinions we form based on the information we have in the moment, are typically how we decide how we communicate with another person. Surprisingly, we operate as if the inferences we make are true.

If we consider the trip to the grocery store and were to communicate with each of the people, we would learn very different truths than the inferences we formed. The truth is the parents with the child running around the store feel so blessed to have a child because the mother was told she would never have children. In fact, they experienced five failed IVF treatments to prove it. It wasn't until the sixth try that they became pregnant. The child they were told would never be was born into the world against all odds. So, if their miracle baby wants to wear pajamas and a cape to the grocery store, they let them. Remember the elderly lady with the woman who you thought was her daughter? The young woman was the elderly lady's caretaker. Her own children no longer speak to her because they blame her for their father's death. And the person standing in front of the chocolate candies wasn't going to buy any. They were there because they recently lost 50 pounds and wanted to face junk food in person and tell it that it no longer had control over them. They were there because they struggled with weight all their life and felt they were finally beating a food addiction.

As is often the case, our inferences are completely wrong. As irrational as it may seem, when we communicate with someone, we are communicating with their perception, which is based on inferences. Perception does not always equal reality. In fact, it rarely does. Perception, or the way we regard, understand, or interpret something, is subjective and often unknown by anyone else other than us. It is also usually never known because we seldom speak our perceptions out loud; however, we still do communicate them without speaking a word. Think about it. If we go back to the person standing in the candy aisle, they may see the eye roll or the look of disgust. Nonverbal language is as equally confusing as verbal language. In this instance, it could mean, "I'm disgusted" or "you're gross." However, the person in the candy aisle could interpret the eye roll or look of disgust as, "You are so sad," or "You will never lose the weight," or "You will die alone and fat." You may wonder how the other person came to those conclusions based on an eye roll. Realize that those are the words they already say to themselves every day and heard growing up as a child. Every time someone stares too long and seems disgusted by their appearance, their degrading self-talk takes over and becomes validated by strangers.

Watzlawick, Beavin, and Jackson advanced the idea that "activity or inactivity, words or silence, all have message value: they influence others and these others, in turn, cannot not respond to these communications and are thus themselves communicating" (pg.1). Therefore, we understand that communication is both active and reactive, and we must develop a communication mindset in order to intentionally engage with another person. Do not let the idea of a communication mindset intimidate you. This is not a complete overhaul of the way you think. I am suggesting that you begin to seek consciously and purposely to understand and then communicate the way you view your set of beliefs and experiences that shape how you make sense of the world and yourself to others.

The fact is that you never know what someone else is going through, experiencing, or telling themselves. Unfortunately, what you see with your eyes only tells you the *what*; it does not tell the *why*. To get to the why, you have to communicate with others.

Getting to the "Why" to Explain the "What"

To clarify, a communication mindset is not about manipulating someone into agreeing with you or proving that you are "right." So, what does it mean? It means that you strive to intentionally be curious and interested in understanding perspective. You are trying to understand the "why" for the "what" that you think you already know. In other words, the "what" can be easy to identify. You can know a woman is a stripper. That's the "what" of the situation. You can see it with your own eyes. But the "why" of the thing is more difficult to see. In this example, it's answering the question: How did stripping become an occupational option? If, as a child, someone's body was sold for drugs, that can land them on a pole. If someone grew up in an environment where they saw that the only way to get money in life is to get it from a man by doing things he likes, that can land someone on a pole. If someone felt hated by their father, had low self-esteem, and longed for the attention of a man, that can land them on a pole.

Remember that we all have a story. We all have an often unknown "why" for the "what" that others see and judge us by. It is the communication mindset that seeks out the why and vacates judgments.

However, the communication mindset often gets impeded by one of three possible factors that aren't in agreement: literal meaning, intended meaning, and perceived meaning. These three elements work together to make communications successful. If one element is "off," communication can break down. See the illustration to better understand how these three elements go into the meaning of communication.

In communication, what is meant often goes beyond what is said. Literal meaning refers to the exact words. Intended meaning refers to our expected or planned meaning of words or a phrase. Perceived meaning refers to our understanding or interpretation of words.

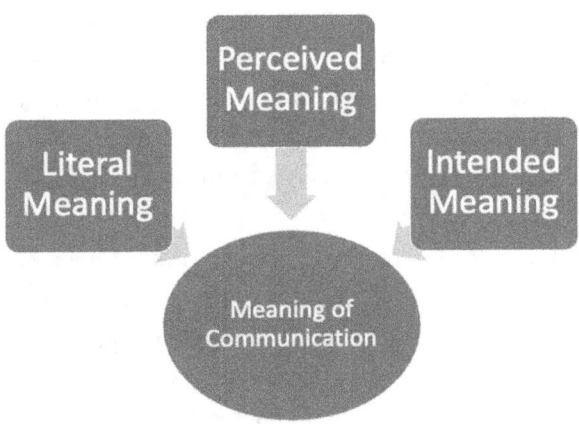

For example, someone can say the words, "I am a recovering addict."

- The literal meaning is that the person had an addiction problem at one time, went through rehab, and is no longer abusing drugs or alcohol.
- The intended meaning of someone saying those words to another person may be that they are in an uncomfortable situation that might lead to relapse, so they are alerting folks around them about their sobriety. There could also be the intention that someone will be empathetic to their situation and ask them if they feel uncomfortable or want to leave.
- The perceived meaning by another person could very well be confusion. Another person may not understand why this "announcement" was made. Or the words could be perceived as "My cousin is a drug addict and I don't believe that anyone can really get clean. They were a recovering addict 12 times before, and the story always ends up the same way—back on drugs."

You can see how easily many things can get missed or misconstrued during communication. This is easy to do. We do this all the time with each other. That's why we need to be mindful and attentive to our thoughts in moments like these. When this happens, it is essential to be open to the possibility that what is in front of you is not what your previous experience has taught you. The shift to a communication mindset means that you identify the moment in time from which you are responding to another person. You communicate, not talk, about your feelings and emotions regarding the situation and how you view the person in the moment. Even more important is to share how previous experiences impacted how you are responding in the moment. When you find yourself in these positions, you may be unsure if it is safe to share your experiences. It is okay to let someone know how you view a situation based on your experience. In fact, you should. How else will they know what is going on in your head? If you do nothing, then the lack of communication continues, and it affects future encounters. One interaction is not just one interaction. Rather, a relationship is formed and based on interactions over the life of the relationship. Every subsequent encounter builds on previous encounters. Is it fair? Not necessarily, but that is what happens.

Realize that communication is a continuum. Unfortunately, most of us believe that we are speaking with a person in the present moment about the present issue; this is usually not the case if there is unresolved tension in the relationship. Think about relationships as being on a timeline. For example, suppose you have a relationship that started in 1980. Let's say in the years 1998 and 2002 some major events happened to you within the confines of that relationship. Here we are today, and your friend asks if you could go with them to visit their grandmother. This seems innocent enough. Except, in 1998, when you went with this friend to visit their grandmother, the uncle who lived with Grandma tried to get you to commit a crime with him. You didn't say anything so as not to upset your friend or the grandmother. You haven't gone back since. You also never mentioned it to anyone. But, in 1998 your friend noticed how you started acting differently toward their grandmother and uncle ever since that visit. They couldn't put their finger on it, but something was different. Since their grandmother was getting up in age, they thought you might want to see her, plus she asked about you. But here is how you can miss each other in the same conversation. You respond to your friend's invite by saying, "No, I won't be able to make it. Your grandmother has cats and I'm allergic." However, your friend thinks you're lying and just giving an excuse not to go. To them, this is just like the time in 2002 when they asked you to go with them to pick up that same uncle who just got released from prison. You made up an excuse not to go then too. Then in 2018, you asked the friend to go with you to take your mother to dialysis. The friend said no. Now you feel that you are in a tit-for-tat friendship (I didn't do something for you and now you won't do something for me). The truth is the friend's grandmother died fairly soon after being put on dialysis. Taking someone else to the same treatment brings up painful memories. But your friend doesn't share that with you, so you assume they are just getting back at you for not going with them to pick up the uncle from prison.

Below is an example of a friendship communication timeline to give you a visual of how this happens over time.

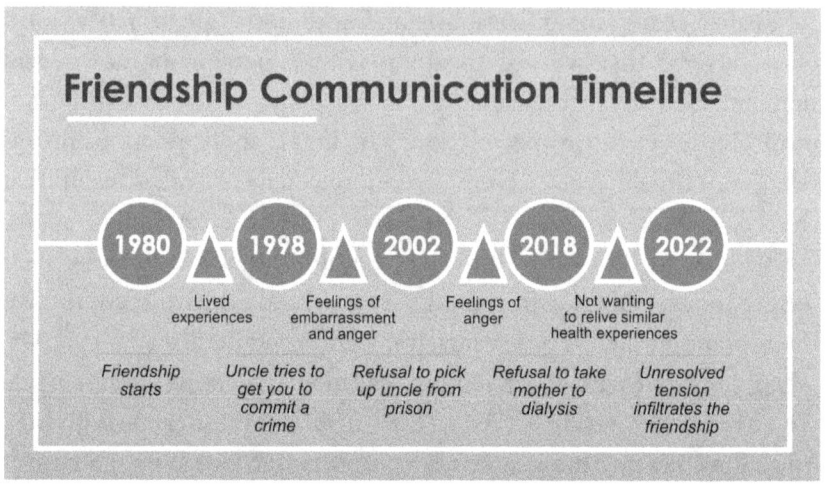

Friendship Communication Timeline

1980	1998	2002	2018	2022
Lived experiences	Feelings of embarrassment and anger	Feelings of anger	Not wanting to relive similar health experiences	
Friendship starts	Uncle tries to get you to commit a crime	Refusal to pick up uncle from prison	Refusal to take mother to dialysis	Unresolved tension infiltrates the friendship

In this moment, many things are happening, but communication between two friends is not one of them. First, we have a friend who doesn't have family to rely on for support with their grandmother. In fact, you have been their friend and family over the years. So, when you don't go with them to deal with family-related issues, they feel unsupported. They also feel like you make judgments about their family and don't really like them. Separately, you feel like the uncle is sketchy and you don't want to be around him. Because he lives with the grandmother, by default you don't want to have anything to do with the grandmother either. Also, you feel that you are always asked to go to deal with family stuff with this friend. You are tired of dealing with the chaos and dysfunction of their family. Your own family has dysfunction, and you don't need to borrow anyone else's dysfunction.

Instead of communication happening, you don't go visit the grandmother and the friend just says "okay." Remember in Chapter 1 we discussed the five ways we attempt to resolve conflict that are not the most effective. Well, here we see a classic example of avoidance. No one is discussing real events or feelings. This situation is now marked on the communication continuum for both of you, and it will affect how you interact in the future.

When you are communicating with someone, you are communicating with all their lived experiences and perceptions that may or may not have anything to do with you. So, it is possible that though you are having a conversation in the present tense, you are actually responding to or dealing with responses based on prior communicative encounters or experiences that span the course of the relationship or over a lifetime.

Moving Beyond Communication Mindset

The idea of developing a communication mindset is what leads us to a Relationship Reset. We just examined real-life situations that most of us find ourselves in at some point. The work we do on ourselves in these situations is what allows us to have the confidence to begin a new relationship with the same person. We aren't expecting people to "act differently." We are not trying to "change" anybody. The hard work we are talking about is on ourselves. The power lies in our ability to develop a communication mindset and function from that space with others. Experiencing a shift in the role we play in personal relationships allows us to be both present and accountable in moments that matter. We are positioned to take ownership of our responses to the events and experiences that happen to us or are caused by us without carrying the weight of keeping taboo topics secret.

Most of us have a weight on us from some of our relationships. This is not healthy for anyone—for you, the other person, and the relationship in general. What we don't realize is that the other person feels this tension too, whether they acknowledge it or not. Just because someone doesn't say something out loud doesn't mean it didn't happen, isn't true, and isn't affecting the relationship. Because it is. The key is learning how to recognize the symptoms this tension causes. The symptoms won't be the same for everyone, and it may not be the same symptom across every relationship. For example, if you are dealing with a mentally ill parent, you may feel anxious and alert every time you are around them. But if you have a friend battling a chronic illness, you may experience feelings of frustration and guilt. While the situations are different, the fact that you experience symptoms is consistent. Since you know you have symptoms, you have to address what to do about them. Let's examine that topic next.

CHAPTER 3

Resolve the Tensions that Permeate Your Relationships

We've discussed that a Relationship Reset, to begin the relationship anew, is necessary for us to resolve the tension in our relationships. At this point, you may be asking yourself, "Why is resetting a relationship important?" That is a fair question. In fact, it makes complete sense to be unsure whether a Relationship Reset is even a "thing." After all, we are all in relationships with friends and family members, so why can't we just leave well enough alone? Even if you have taboo topics in the relationship, you may have already normalized not talking about it, so why "rock the boat"? In fact, in some relationships, you may have even gone so far as to act as if "the event" never happened. At the very least, you may feel that you are at least talking to each other, albeit superficially, and that is better than what it used to be. Plus, you may feel there is nothing you can or should do to improve the way you interact with each other.

Well, here's the truth: Even if you know there are things that you don't talk about anymore with someone, and you believe you have moved past it, chances are that you have not, in fact, moved past it. Or maybe one person has moved past it and one person hasn't. It could also be that one or both of you are at different stages of trying to resolve what happened. And this, my friends, is why you should intentionally seek to have the same understanding about the relationship. You see, the relationship you have now is the relationship you will have in the future. Unless you put in intentional effort to work on yourself *and* on the relationship, your strained relationship will just drift along and be subject to whatever and whoever comes along, without guideposts.

The Symptoms of Tension are Our Guideposts

When you hear the word "guideposts," you may think of rules. That's not really what I'm referring to here. For our purposes, "guideposts" are those symptoms within a relationship that certain events trigger. In Chapter 2 we learned why we need to develop a communication mindset to be able to initiate a Relationship Reset. We also learned that there are symptoms that go along with the tension that exists in our relationships. As we discussed before, situations happen all the time that affect us directly, and in turn, they affect our relationship with other people. Often, we don't realize what is happening, and if we do, we may choose to ignore it. We might feel the emotion from it, but we don't address it. We let the feelings go, thinking that we don't want to make a big deal out of something or cause an argument. Or we try to explain it away, as if it's not what we think it is.

Those feelings and those emotions are our guideposts. These guideposts give us direction. They let us know that there is a path ahead. While the path in front of us may be unknown, we are pointed in a direction. The symptoms that we experience because of the tension are what guides us in the same way.

The benefit of guideposts is that they tell us what we need to communicate in the moment. Guideposts are based on what is going on inside of us that is invisible to others. They are our feelings, emotions, experiences, and perspectives that we would not normally discuss; however, they alert us of the opportunity to connect with another person that we are in a close relationship with. Guideposts are the thoughts we might have, such as, "Oh my gosh, you are still doing this after all these years?" or "I should tell the truth about what really happened." This is very different from the social advice you may have heard that goes: "If you don't have anything nice to say, don't say anything at all." The difference is in the kind of relationship we are talking about as well as the relational goals. When embarking on a Relationship Reset, we are talking about working on a relationship that has history and the sharing of personal experiences. For a reset to take place and for the guideposts to matter, the relationship has to matter. Further, the goal of the relationship should be to resolve the tension, make the relationship better, and encourage closeness. This is a relationship that we want to be better.

If you had to think about a personal relationship where you experience symptoms from the tension, which one would you pick? Most of us know exactly which relationship it is and how long the tension has existed. Think about the last time you thought about *not* bringing the taboo topic up. Were you talking to a friend? Your dad? Your cousin? How did you feel after the encounter when you did not communicate your feelings? I imagine it's not very good. And guess what? These unresolved feelings usually show up repeatedly, when you least expect it, and impact not just you, but also the relationship.

When you fail to communicate, the issue doesn't disappear. On the contrary, it festers, causing even worse symptoms. As time passes and the years drag on, so does the tension. Despite the old adage, time, by itself, does not heal anything.

So, what's the solution? How do we use our guideposts to move toward the Relationship Reset? First, you need to identify the source of the symptoms. Ask yourself, "Where is the tension really coming from?" Is the tension from the context of the relationship? Or from other experiences that you have allowed to infect this relationship? Is the tension from the present moment? Or is it from somewhere along the communication continuum? Remember, we discussed that communication flows along a timeline, and it is very possible to have unresolved tension from months or even years ago with this person.

Everything we are learning about is based in communication, but some of this is part psychology, because this process requires us to be honest with ourselves about the truths that exist in the dark corners of our mind. While I am not a psychologist, therapist, counselor, or psychiatrist, I believe there is value in spending time "on the couch." Mental health is health. All components of your health matter: emotional, spiritual, mental, physical, financial, relational –all of it affects your wellbeing. Dealing with the tension you have in relationships or among family members may require professional support to help you discern the origin of the tension and understand how it affects your life.

The source of the tension can be from an internal or external influence. What's the difference? Well, internal influence means that whatever is causing the tension happened over the course of the relationship involving the people within the relationship. External influence implies that the tension is caused by something or someone that has nothing to do with the relationship, but the tension is infecting the relationship.

Let's put this in perspective and revisit the earlier discussion about the affair. You may be avoiding the friend because the two of you made a pact years ago, when you each got married, that you would never cheat, and now it feels like it was all just a lie. That's an internal influence. Or you may be avoiding the friend because you had an affair years ago, and seeing your friend do the same thing reminds you of your misdeeds. That's also internal. Think about internal as self-imposed—something you do or say to yourself. Your self-talk can create the tension. Now, if the friend demands you keep certain secrets from other friends or family members regarding the affair, that's external. It is something or someone acting upon you. When these types of issues happen, what do you do? Do you acquiesce because it seems easier? But the question is, easier than what? And easier for whom? You likely don't even know what the alternative would be. You may think you know what will be said and how the situation will unfold. But you really don't. There are more questions than answers.

These are the tough questions we all must manage constantly. Even more important, these are questions you are likely asking yourself. This has nothing to do with the other person and has everything to do with you. The source of why you feel the way you do about the topic is important. This understanding is necessary to finally start the reset process. If you are going to start something anew, you have to be willing to tear down the old system.

Most times, the old system we operate from is based on how we interpret and function in the world around us, and the people in our close circles learn to work around it. Why do they do that? Because they love us. They think they are showing love by not upsetting us, not creating a problem where there isn't one. So we make workarounds, adjustments, and changes to accommodate the system and to maintain the system. Somewhere along the way we become more committed to the system than to the friendship.

Because we have long-term relationships, we respond based on the information we know. Let's go back to the example of the affair and let's observe the situation from afar, as a bystander. It is very likely that both people have a history of cheating on their spouse and have developed a system in the friendship to accommodate cheating. They have worked out signals and created a code to use. For example, if one receives a call from the other, they know to say, "What time are we meeting up for drinks?" That is code for "My spouse is listening to this call. I'm saying this out loud in earshot, so you know that I am going out for the night. If you get a call or a text looking for me, you know where I'm at and who I'm with." You may think this sounds wild, but this is how many people "do" relationships.

For a system to exist, whatever the system is, there must be people and structures in place that promote the system. There must be mutual communication of understanding. That is the only way the system works. Relationships work in the same way. Relationships exist in whatever condition they are in because we fight to maintain the system, regardless if it's dysfunctional, unhealthy, toxic, or unsafe. Given that reality, the only way for a relationship to function differently is for the system to be reset.

The Reset

I have to be honest and admit that initiating a Relationship Reset can be messy because we are disrupting the status quo of how the relationship works. You are disrupting the system. Most people in relationships play a role, whether they want to admit it or not. Often, we didn't choose the role; it just befell upon us in the context and circumstances of the relationship. For example, you may be the "mother" who always gives advice and direction. You may be the "caretaker" who makes sure the person takes their medications or stays sober. You may be the "protector" who is always present for family functions to protect a friend from the toxic relationship with their mother. By no means is this an exhaustive list, as there are many roles we can play in families and in relationships. However, when the roles suddenly change, pushback occurs.

Establishing a new normal for the relationship may seem like a daunting task and something that seems impossible quite frankly. You are setting new rules and boundaries, which may mean there is a change in the roles. In fact, some roles could be eliminated completely. To some people, saying that people have roles in a relationship means that we are acting to an extent. That's fair. But consider this: Acting is not real, so that means there are parts of the relationship that may not be real. The reset is a way to stop the acting. It allows us to function as our authentic selves in the relationship in a way that builds upon what already exists.

When you embark on a Relationship Reset, you are accepting that the way the relationship used to function, or the role you used to play, is no more. While it may seem counterintuitive to put on your oxygen mask first before assisting others, it is not admirable for two people to die unnecessarily. In the context of a relationship, it does not make sense for those in the relationship to suffer with the emotional baggage that goes along with taboo topics that are infecting the relationship.

For true change, you have to first tear the relationship down. This idea may sound destructive. That's because it is. You are tearing down your preconceived notions about how you feel about what has happened in the past. You are tearing down the wall of secrecy and stigma that has been built around the taboo topic. But here's what you are not doing: You are not starting an argument. This is not an attack or an ambush. Remember, you are working on developing your communication mindset. You are approaching the person and the taboo topic differently. Why? Because what you have been doing isn't working. This isn't about casting blame. It's not your fault that your past approaches haven't worked. Remember, you learned communication skills passively and from external forces.

In the following chapter we will discuss key reasons why many of us keep fumbling in this area of relationships. We are going to discuss communication roadblocks that prevent us from being the best communicators we can be. Then, we will sift through the rubble after the relational tear down to work through what makes sense to salvage. Part of that process will also involve finding the courage to move forward. As you can imagine, this part of the process will require a lot of effort from both people involved to be successful, but it can be done. You will get to the other side of this and be in a better place than you are now. You will be stronger, because you will be armed with tools that will allow you to focus on the power of the strengths in the relationship and in the other person. It is those strengths that will keep you grounded in the commitment to the relationship and one another, as opposed to being committed to the system.

Finally, we will discuss relationship endings. Though not ideal, sometimes it makes the most sense for people to no longer be in contact with one another. Certainly, stopping all communication may not be a mutual decision; however, it is a decision that should be considered and respected if chosen.

While it might seem like this work is all about the other person, you are really focusing on yourself. You have a responsibility to yourself and the other person to right any past wrongs, admit your true experiences, and decide to have a new relationship that moves forward in a new and better direction.

PART 2

CREATING THE RELATIONSHIPS YOU REALLY WANT

CHAPTER 4

Remove the Roadblocks to Effective Communication

As we have learned, communication is not inherently easy nor is it something that just happens. Most of us don't get relationships right because of the common roadblocks that make communication feel like an obstacle course at times. To effectively communicate, we have to first identify the roadblocks. But the problem with roadblocks is that we often don't recognize them. They can appear as truths because we have normalized them.

Roadblocks prohibit us from being vulnerable to the communication process with another. They create "mixed messages" about information that we try to convey. Mixed messages are when we have thoughts or feelings that are very different from each other about the same thing. For example, if you were to get angry at a friend for not staying in rehab, yet you dropped out of college in your sophomore year, you could be giving a mixed message. While these are not the same things exactly, the other person can view the situation as "the pot calling the kettle black." This is not to say the other person is right or that the two events are comparable; however, people do think in this way. The fact is that we are not all going to think the same way or have the same experiences, which is a good thing. The problem is that many people view differences as means for divisions. But diversity of thought, people, and experiences foster such a rich environment for relationships. Unfortunately, we can miss the opportunities for a relationship because we oftentimes focus on the roadblocks instead of the person and the circumstances of the present situation.

These roadblocks exist internally and externally to all of us. Internal roadblocks have to do with how our perceptions and experiences shape how we function in a relationship and the expectations we have for relationships. External roadblocks are outside influences that we do not necessarily control; however, they have profound impact on the way we operate in a relationship and can even alter our interactions with another person. In total, I've identified seven communication roadblocks. First, we'll examine the four internal roadblocks more closely, and then we'll turn to the three external roadblocks to understand their significance to the communication process.

The Four Internal Roadblocks

1. Honesty

You may be wondering how honesty can serve as a roadblock. If anything, it should encourage communication. Interestingly, in tempting situations, honesty may require deliberation. Honesty can also be subjective. How can that be? After all, honesty seems straight forward; either someone is honest or they're not. Either what someone says is the truth or it's not. Unfortunately, many variations of how to define honesty exist. Think about it. What is a lie? What is a white lie? Is there a difference between the two? What about omitting certain facts? Is that lying? Is there such a thing as half-truths? What about being honest, but not *honest-honest?* Where does deception fit into all of this? As you can see, "gray areas" of honesty are very real. Most of us do not think about the nuance and detail until someone is functioning in what we perceive as a gray area.

For example, let's think about honesty in the realm of infidelity. A wife asks her husband, "Where were you last night? I was worried when I didn't hear from you before I went to sleep. What were you doing out so late?" The husband replies, "You know I was out with Eric and them. Then Michael came to meet us, and he had some friends with him. You know how that goes." Now, this may seem like a very reasonable answer. It makes sense. But when naming all the friends who showed up, the husband forgot to mention that Tiffany also showed up. Tiffany is the mistress. Did he flat out lie to his wife?

Did he just omit facts? Depending on your personal experiences and outlook, maybe … or maybe not.

Think about the last time you either told a lie or felt that someone lied to you. What exactly made it a lie? Did the other person also think it was a lie? Much like communication, honesty exists on a continuum. You might not admit it, but sometimes you can determine the degree of honesty based on the source. For example, are you more likely to believe information that comes from your cousin or your mother? You may not be able to answer that, because it could also depend on the information. If your cousin tells you that they are struggling with infertility, you may be inclined to believe it with the understanding that they have been trying to get pregnant but have been unable to because of some medical reason. But if your mother tells you that your cousin is struggling with infertility, you may be inclined to not believe her and think she is telling you this with the hope that you will ask your cousin about it and then report back to your mother about what you found out. See the difference in how "honesty" can be used by different people and for different reasons?

Because of this very gray area in which honesty can exist, we need to understand that the most important degree of honesty is the honesty we have with ourselves. Subsequently, we must then communicate that honesty about the taboo topic.

Regarding your relationships and the taboo topics that are unaddressed, consider if you have been truly honest about your feelings, position, or attitude in the situation, and honest about how you view the other person. Have you been totally honest with the other person? Specifically, reflect whether you have communicated how you have perceived the person's actions, words, or behaviors in the situation. The greatest strength you have is your honesty with another person about how all these truths have affected you and thus the relationship. Equally important is to be honest about how your response in a situation is directly related to those truths.

You may be wondering how to get to this honesty. Let's consider the following situation: You witness a friend's significant other out in a restaurant eating dinner with a person who is not your friend. You think you might be catching them cheating in the act! What do you do? How do you respond? This is the time when you have to be honest with yourself. Honesty really matters in this situation, because it will determine what you do with what you just witnessed. You can formulate all sorts of justifications for what you do next, but none of it will matter if it isn't grounded in honesty. You can tell the friend about what you saw and even take pictures to prove it. Or you can decide to say nothing and act as if you didn't see anything. Either way, you have to be honest with yourself about why you made the choice to tell or not tell. Did you tell because you knew the person's significant other was a total loser all along and this was a great opportunity to prove your point? Did you not tell because you know what it feels like when someone tells you this and you don't want to hurt your friend in this way? Think about it this way: if you ever had to explain your decision of why you did or did not tell, what would you say? Whatever that is, that is your honesty.

Here are some questions for you to ponder about honesty:

1. How do I define honesty?
2. How have I communicated my definition of honesty to others?
3. How do I need to communicate honesty to others moving forward?

Now that we have pondered over a few questions, an even bigger question to ask is: "How do I get around the roadblock?" If you feel you want to move to a space of honesty, definitely start by working through the questions listed above. When you think about how you define honesty, also consider where you learned honesty. Who taught you about honesty? How did you arrive at your definition for honesty? If you are having a difficult time defining honesty, that is a clear sign that you still have some work to do on yourself. After all, if you aren't sure how you define honesty, you may not know it when you see it. Likewise, you may have a hard time identifying dishonesty in others as well.

Next, consider the ways you have communicated honesty to others, either through words or deeds. How you have shown honesty to others is likely how you interpret honesty in others. For example, if a cousin asks you to pick up something from the store for them and they will pay you back for it, you may make sure you have the receipt to show your honesty. Even though you have never given your cousin reason to believe you might steal from them or lie about the cost of the item, you are most comfortable taking steps to ensure no one could ever view you as a thief. This is you in action defining honesty.

Once you are clear about how you define honesty and how you communicate honesty to others, it's time to move beyond talk and put it into action to reset the relationship. A very authentic way to communicate your honesty with another person is to make it very plain. This is not the time to use big words. This is the time to be your authentic self. Remember, you are sharing information you have not shared with this person before. You might say, "I have not been honest with you about this issue in part because I wasn't sure what honesty really meant to me. Now I know that honesty for me means that I will not withhold information from you. With that said, I need to be honest with you right now…"

2. Apprehension

You might be afraid or have anxiety associated with the idea of either real or anticipated communication with another person or persons. This is communication apprehension. I extend the definition to include the factor that creates the anxiety. In this instance, the taboo topic. At its very core, communication apprehension is a psychological response to how we evaluate a communicative encounter. This psychological response, however, quickly becomes physical as our body responds to the threat the mind perceives. The human body cannot distinguish between psychological and physical threats, so we respond as though we are getting physically attacked. In earlier chapters, we discussed that sometimes we may feel sweaty, or our heart may start beating fast, or we may feel anxious at the thought of the taboo topic. That is communication apprehension.

This happens because the body's circulatory and adrenal systems shift into overdrive, preparing us to function at maximum physical efficiency—the "flight or fight" response. Yet instead of running away or fighting, we usually just stand there (or sit down) and try to endure the situation. This is ineffective for helping us improve our communication and resolve the strain of the taboo topic infecting the relationship. Trying to manage the apprehension going on within us around a particular topic can be difficult because we are juggling both the physical and psychological response. These physical reactions to stress create the uncomfortable feelings of unease called speech anxiety and may include sweaty palms, increased heart rate, butterflies in the stomach, the need to use the restroom, and dry mouth.

When these symptoms occur, you may shut down because you think you know how the other person is going to respond, based on past experiences. Or you may shut down because you have no idea how the person will react, and that's scary too. Or you may think the news is so damaging or regretful that you will never be forgiven for sharing it. All of that may be true, but by not addressing the situation and facing the person armed with the truth, you are allowing this taboo topic to have control over you and over the relationship.

For example, if you were to reveal to your child that you have been diagnosed with a mental illness, that can certainly create communication apprehension. What if you were diagnosed years ago and have been trying to hide it, but you have reached a point where the doctor thinks inpatient treatment is necessary? Of course, you are worried about what the other side of treatment looks like. Will your child still love you? Will they support you? What will it do to the relationship? You may also have feelings of guilt for not sharing the diagnosis earlier and putting your child through all the mental breakdowns and erratic episodes without explanation. You feel that you made their life harder than it needed to be. All these questions and concerns are perfectly normal to have and surely warrant being apprehensive about communicating.

With that in mind, realize that the issues that cause apprehension are the topics we should confront, not stray away from. Here are some questions to ponder about apprehension:

1. Create an inventory of the physiological symptoms of communication apprehension you experience around a particular subject. Which topics in the conversation cause the symptoms?
2. How have I responded with my words when facing the issues that give me apprehension?
3. What makes me relieved of the symptoms?

As you consider the questions about apprehension, reflect on a particular encounter you have had with someone in the past. Then, think about encounters with different people. Were the physiological symptoms the same? Did the symptoms change depending on the topic? When you have moved through the exercise of writing down the symptoms you experienced, with whom, and the topics discussed, think about your response. What did you say or not say but wished you did in those situations? What did you do or not do but wish you had? Now, note when you have felt relief from the symptoms. What happened? What gave you relief?

To avoid having apprehension become a roadblock to your communication, you must first identify the symptoms and what causes them. Usually, relief comes when you face the fear. I can assure you that most of the time, what you imagined to be the outcome is just that—imaginary. You have no way of knowing how a situation will turn out, especially when you are trying something new. That's why you have the apprehension in the first place. You are afraid of the outcome. Eliminating the fear through action is the only way to overcome the roadblock.

3. Judgment

We all judge and have been judged. We know it's not right, yet we make judgments about people and situations all the time. Technically, judgments are defined as decisions or opinions people reach after careful consideration. Interestingly, most of us do not apply "careful consideration;" rather, we often make snap judgments, and we don't let them go. That judgment then becomes what we believe. We usually make these judgments in our mind and do not necessarily verbalize them.

In the context of a relationship, judgments can be very dangerous because they guide our thoughts and actions. Even if we don't explicitly speak our judgments out loud, our actions reveal what we think. Let's consider if an uncle has suffered with a drinking problem for many years, yet the family acts as if there is not a problem. You might make a judgment about the uncle and believe that he has been a drunk all his life, does not want help, and will never change.

We establish judgments to make sense of what is going on around us. Often, we make these judgments through the lens of opinions and rarely include facts (or not all the facts). The problem with this process is that we seldom communicate the judgment to the person we are judging. In our eyes, the person becomes known by the judgment rather than their actual self. They become a label. In this case, the uncle becomes "the drunk," no longer seen as the little boy who watched his father drink himself into an early grave.

We have all been subject to judgments in relationships, unknowingly or knowingly. I am sure the opinions did not seem fair, or at the very least were not grounded in all the facts. Unfortunately, we all can pass judgments on others, especially those closest to us. This becomes problematic around the issues of taboo topics, because those judgments can prevent us from moving forward. Think about a time when you were judged. What did you want to do most? I imagine you wanted to defend yourself if you felt the judgment wasn't true or explain yourself if some of it or all of it was true. Whatever the situation, I imagine these judgments made communication much more complicated.

Here is an example of how judgments become roadblocks in our communication about taboo topics in close relationships. Let's say your father was diagnosed with diabetes type II and subsequently lost his leg due to the progression of the disease. He now expects you to manage all his health care. So you drive him back and forth to the medical appointments, go to the pharmacy for him, spend hours on the phone with insurance companies and physical therapists … the list goes on. You were not expecting him to lose his leg, nor did you expect to take on this role at this point in your life; you are still raising your own family. Despite all of this, you judge your father for all his "bad health." You watched him not take care of his health for years, even when the doctors told him if he did not change his lifestyle and take his medication as directed, it would lead to losing his leg and possibly blindness. He was aware of where this was headed, yet here you both are. You judge your dad for what has happened. In your mind, this is all his fault. If only he had exercised, taken his medication, and followed the doctor's advice, he would not be in this situation. Further, you would not be burdened as the surrogate caretaker if he had taken better care of his health.

As a result of his untimely health events and the subsequent judgments you made about him, the relationship has become broken. In fact, there really isn't a relationship anymore. The new patient and caretaker roles have replaced what used to be movie nights and trips to the driving range. But you don't communicate any of this because judgments have infected the relationship.

As you move toward being more aware of your judgments, consider the following questions. As you do, think about judgments you have made about someone and how that affected your communication.

1. What judgments have I made about the person and/or the situation? What has informed my judgment?

2. Are the judgments fair and balanced? What (provable) facts do I have about the situation?

3. How do I minimize/remove judgments about the person/situation moving forward?

Interestingly, judgments provide more insight into the person making them than the person they are about. As we work through the questions, the first one allows us to come to terms with the judgments we have made about individuals or situations. Then we determine if the judgment is fair. As we mentioned earlier, judgments are not fair. That doesn't mean we made them up out of thin air. Often, we make judgments based on something someone said or did or what we believe someone said or did.

This brings us to the all-important question: How do we stop making judgments? The truth is, you don't completely stop. Your lived experiences give you a roadmap of sorts to follow in order to make decisions that are in your best interest. With that in mind, to minimize the roadblock that judgments can put in your communication, you need to first be aware that you have them and then understand why you have them. Also, try to substantiate your judgment. If you can't, should you maintain the judgment?

If we take the example of the father who suffered an amputation, it would be helpful to share with him that while no one expected this to happen and it is a painful experience, the caregiving has been exhausting. Of course, no one wants to have an amputation and certainly doesn't plan for their child to become their primary caretaker. In this instance, you can confront your judgment that your father could have prevented this from happening by asking questions. You can start with, "Dad, how do you think losing a leg happens to people with diabetes?" or "In what ways has losing your leg affected your life and your health?" You may be surprised by the answers.

4. Stigmata (stigma)

The definition of stigma has some variability; however, at its very core, stigma represents the mark of disgrace that links a person to undesirable and devalued characteristics and is associated with a particular circumstance, quality, or person. Living under a stigma can be self-imposed, socially imposed, or culturally imposed. Regardless of their origin, stigmas can create feelings of shame, guilt, hate, etc. We all have very clear opinions about what we perceive to be stigmatizing issues. Unfortunately, all stigma is not created equally and can be subjective. What is equally understood though is the separation or strain the stigma creates. The only way to eliminate a stigma is to destigmatize it.

How do we do that? To begin, we must bring the issue to the light. Too often, these types of issues are buried, considered dirty, and kept in the dark. Most of us don't initiate these types of conversations because we have branded them. And once branded, it is hard to remove the brand because it becomes an identity. Jane becomes "the person with one leg." Mark is now "the guy whose wife is in prison." We give people labels so casually that it becomes a habit. We don't think about how inconsiderate this practice is, and usually the person we are referring to doesn't say anything about it, so we go along as if it is acceptable. This is an awful way to refer to someone.

If someone used a label every time they referred to you, how would you feel? How would that affect how you interacted with someone? You are no longer considered an individual with feelings, emotions, and dreams; rather, this "thing" that happened to you has become your identity because that is how others view you. This is unfair, mean, inconsiderate, and causes greater harm.

We can't always prevent or avoid situations from occurring, particularly the shameful and stigmatizing events. There has to be a space for grace, healing, and shedding of the stigma. Unfortunately, for these types of situations to make sense to us, we assign blame on the person. What is interesting and often overlooked about blame is that we are quick to assign it to others, yet we must remember that we all make mistakes—often.

You can't have effective and heartfelt communication in a personal relationship when you hold a perspective that stigmatizes the other person. Regardless of what happened, how it happened, or the aftermath caused by it, you must move past the event causing the stigma and deal with who remains, which is your friend, your brother, your aunt, etc.

For example, as a society we should be able to discuss mental illness as easily as we discuss diabetes or a heart attack. But we do not. We place a stigma on such things as a mental health diagnosis and drug use. Why? Why does someone "commit suicide" but another person "dies from a heart attack?" Both situations are very tragic and result from disease. Yet suicide creates stigma and the feeling of embarrassment or shame for those related to or close to the person who passed. And it shouldn't.

In personal relationships, you need to figure out how you formed any stigmatizing opinions and then unpack how they affect your relationships, because they do. Whether you acknowledge it or not, issues that you view as stigmatizing impact personal relationships because they influence how you view the other person and subsequently interact with them.

Here are some questions to ponder about stigma:

1. What stigma(s) do I hold against a person and/or a situation?
2. What has informed my formation of these stigma(s)?
3. What steps do I take to acknowledge/eradicate my stigma?

Stigmas are difficult to overcome but you can take the power out of them. You can control whether you accept and propagate stigma or whether you take steps to destigmatize it. Remember, stigmas only exist because people create them and perpetuate them. When you have identified the stigmas and understand where they came from, then you are on a path to ending them. Whether you impart stigma on yourself or other people, you have to normalize the stigmatized issue. If you keep the stigma secret or hidden, you are allowing it to persist. You have to communicate about the stigma to get rid of the roadblock.

The Three External Roadblocks

We just reviewed four internal roadblocks to communication. Of course, this is not an exhaustive list, but it does give us insight into how our communication gets hampered from things going on inside of us.

Let's now move on to the three external roadblocks. These are the things happening around us that affect our communication in personal relationships. External roadblocks are issues that occur outside of our control. We may perceive them as happening "to us" and feel unable to change the situation/circumstances.

1. Social influence

Social influence refers to the way in which we change our ideas and actions to meet the expectations of a social group, perceived authority, or social role. In other words, we want to fit in. This is an interesting idea for us to think about regarding communication. Most of us are aware of social influence. We are subject to it every day via email, social media, cell phones, etc. But few people have thought about how it plays out in personal relationships.

For example, your best friend calls you and asks you to go with them to a party. Because you know how this friend parties, you know there will be excessive drinking, wild sex, and drugs at this party. Your friend knows you don't drink, have sex in public, or do drugs, but they still invited you. They also mentioned several other friends who are going. They want you to be the designated driver. You usually serve in this role but lately you feel the parties have gotten more out of control, and your friend's behavior has become more erratic at these parties. You don't mind being the trusted designated driver, but it's getting old. Because several friends are going, they are each separately calling you to go to the party. This is how social influence plays out in our everyday lives. It's so normal and can seem subtle, but it can have a great impact on how we interact with each other. You might just go along with what everyone else wants because it's easier. But if you are simply going along, that means you are not communicating how you feel. Instead, the feelings fester and continue to multiply over weeks, months, and years, turning to resentment and slowly decaying the friendship along with it.

Think about the last time someone or several close friends or family members tried to get you to do something that you were not comfortable doing. What did you do? How did it make you feel? How did it affect the relationship?

If you've ever felt the pressure of social influence, you may be wondering how you let it happen. "Am I just not strong enough to say no?" That is not it. Willpower alone is not sufficient. There are several reasons why we allow social influences to affect our thoughts and behavior and ultimately the way we communicate in our personal relationships. One reason is that we conform to the norms of a group to gain acceptance. We want to belong to this friend group or family group, so we readily accept their rules. Another reason involves the concept of "group think." When this happens, we tend to have the same beliefs as those in the group and reject criticism from those who oppose or question the group's behavior. In essence, we no longer think for ourselves; rather, we defer to the group for decisions.

In either instance, social influence is clear. So the question should not be, "How does this happen?" Rather, ask, "How do I check in with myself on how social influence affects my opinions and behaviors? Are my opinions really my own?" Be honest with yourself (which we learned earlier can be difficult to do) about how your ability to communicate in personal relationships has been influenced by these things. You should be able to discern your beliefs from social beliefs.

Here are some questions to ponder around social influence.

1. Which social groups do I belong to?
2. How have those social groups influenced my beliefs and behaviors?
3. How have I communicated my beliefs as a member of these groups?

Reflecting on your own social beliefs gives you great perspective on the social groups you belong to and how these groups shape your beliefs and behaviors. To not allow social groups to be a roadblock to how you communicate, you have to first understand what they are. Then you must decide to think for yourself. This isn't to imply that you cut off all social networks; that would be ridiculous. However, you do need to be careful you aren't losing your own thoughts and decisions to those around you. When you are unable to convey your own thoughts and ideas, you hinder the communication process.

2. Family dynamics

Family dynamics is a term used to describe how family members interact with one another. Family systems have certain parts, roles, or functions that can create patterns of behavior for everyone in the family. Interestingly, the family can have a great impact on how we interact in personal relationships. That's because the family is our first experience with other people in a personal context. As the system changes, so does our sense of how to engage with people. Within a family there are many relationships: parents, siblings, aunts, uncles, grandparents, cousins, nieces, nephews, co-parenting relationships, and extended family. There are also family roles: rescuer, hero, mediator, lost child, thinker, powerbroker, scapegoat, and clown, to name just a few. We also have family structures: nuclear family, divorced parents, adoptive parents, same-sex parents, blended families, and more. All these variations of how a family is formed and functions are the foundation for our future relationships. In our families is where we learn how to talk, walk, and act. We learn the rules of life and what is and is not acceptable to do or say.

I just mentioned several roles that can exist within a family: rescuer, hero, mediator, lost child, thinker, powerbroker, scapegoat, and clown. Though not exhaustive, this list gives you an idea of how the way we function in a family can affect how we function in relationships outside of the family. It also provides great insight into how we learn to communicate. Here is a brief description of each role to give you a sense of where you might fit along the family role spectrum:

Rescuer: The rescuer takes care of others' needs and emotions, and problem-solves for others in the family.

Hero: This is the "good" and "responsible" one. This person carries the pride of the family.

Mediator: The mediator can be a rescuer-type, although they work to keep peace in the family system. This person does the emotional work of the family to avoid conflict.

Lost child: The lost child is the subservient good child. They are obedient, passive, and hidden in the family trauma. They stay hidden to avoid being a problem.

Thinker: The thinker provides the objective, reasoning focus.

Power broker: This person works at maintaining a hierarchy in the family with the power broker at the top.

Scapegoat: This is the person the other family members feel needs the most help. Usually this is the family member that might do drugs or commit illegal acts. This person often shows the obvious symptoms of the family being unable to work through problems.

Clown: The clown uses humor to offset the family conflict and to create a sense that things are okay even if they are not.

In addition to family roles, families also have communication patterns. We can either have a family that encourages everyone to discuss a variety of diverse topics, or we can have a family that believes communication should emphasize similarity. Overall, most families fit into one of four types of patterns: consensual families, pluralistic families, protective families, or laissez-faire families. Let's look at each from the perspective of a very common family question: Where should we go for dinner?

Families with a consensual type of communication value open conversation, but also conformity within the family unit. Family members communicate freely about thoughts, feelings, and activities, but at the same time, parents are the final decision-makers about important issues. In this family communication pattern, everyone will share their opinions and give reasons why one restaurant should be picked over another, but ultimately, the parent will decide.

Pluralistic families are oriented toward conversation. Parents in these families believe in the value of "life lessons," and they expect their children to develop through their interactions with people outside the family unit. They make decisions as a family, with everyone having equal input. These families also engage in open conflict resolution. They are not afraid of disagreements and have developed good strategies to resolve differences. In this family communication pattern, everyone will share their opinions and give reasons why one restaurant should be picked over another, and they will argue back and forth over the best dinner spot. Typically, this family strives to make decisions as a family.

Protective families do not value open conversation and are oriented toward conformity. In these families, members are likely to hear the parent say, "Because I said so." Parents do not usually share the reasoning for their decisions. In this family communication pattern, the parents will simply say, "Get ready. We are going out for dinner tonight."

Laissez-faire families don't really value conversation or conformity. Family members are often described as "emotionally divorced" from one another. Not much is discussed among members of the family, and parents often don't have an interest or investment in the decisions their children make. Everyone functions independent of one another. In this family structure, going out to eat together may not even be a thing. More likely, everyone is on their own to figure out dinner.

If you want to change the dynamics of your family, you need to understand how these subsystems work and what function each one plays in the system. Most family systems fight for survival, whether it is dysfunctional, healthy, happy, chaotic, or seemingly non-existent.

Here are some questions to ponder about family dynamics:

1. What family communication pattern most resembles my family?
2. What is my role in my family?
3. How has my family communication pattern affected my personal relationships?

As you think about the role you have in your family and the communication pattern you have grown up in, you should also focus on how that has hindered your communication. In order to prevent family dynamics from being a roadblock to your communication, you have to decide who you want to be, not just how you have been viewed in the context of your family. Think about it ... someone who is the clown in their family does not have to function as the clown in personal relationships. While this is easier said than done, it is important to understand whether you have defined how you function in relationships versus simply accepting the role you have been assigned. Ultimately, you may not be able to change how your family communicates, as the patterns can be deeply entrenched and can date back for generations, but you can change how you choose to communicate and function within them.

3. Power

In its most basic definition, power is the ability to influence or control people and events. You may be thinking, "I don't have 'power' in my personal relationships." But you do. Power is one of the most interesting yet mischaracterized dynamics that can exist in personal relationships. You may also be thinking, "No one has 'power' over me. I am an adult. I am in a relationship with who I want to be in a relationship with—I make those decisions." That may be true. Or it may be partly true. Power is a currency. In fact, we can identify five power currencies that exist: Resource Currency, Expertise Currency, Social Network Currency, Personal Currency, and Intimacy Currency.

- Resource currency is when someone possesses material things that someone else needs or wants. Think money, property, food, etc.
- Expertise currency is when someone has knowledge or a highly specialized skill.
- Social network currency is the personal assets and attributes of an individual that help them succeed in interactive social channels.
- Personal Currency is one way of getting needs met by using what we are born with, or what we have cultivated in our lives, to get what we want.
- Intimacy currency is when you share a close bond with someone else that no one else has power over.

You may not think of currency in this way or as a form of power, which is why it's important to understand it and its profound effect on relationships. Why? Because its impact on how we communicate can hinder our communication. Each way in which currency exists, a power dynamic also exists. What's interesting about power is that it only exists if we grant it permission to exist. What do I mean? Take a simple example like a traffic light. Everyone with a driver's license understands the significance of traffic lights. Having said that, if the people in an entire city or state decided they would no longer stop at red lights, then the local traffic and police would no longer have power over its citizens. In the same way there is power in a traffic light, there is power in personal relationships.

Different currencies can affect how we communicate, or not, in relationships. Think about social network currency. Currently, social media is the gold standard by which people connect. If we consider the currency of social media, it indeed is a means by which others seek promotion and opportunities. If someone makes contact through social media, they have a goal in mind. Whether they want to reconnect with an old high school friend, search for a long-lost love, or seek business opportunities, there is a goal. The issues usually arise when the intent for connection is not clear, or the ask is not communicated. The person seeking the connection often perceives the power the other holds. This does not mean that the person with the social network currency is yielding power over another person, but it does mean that because another person sees them as valuable, a power structure exists. For example, if someone reaches out to another person to serve as a mentor because they want to start a business, the budding entrepreneur might be more willing to comply with the potential mentor's requests. Again, this is because the new entrepreneur would feel that the mentor has some degree of power. Does that affect the dynamics of communication? It certainly can. The budding entrepreneur may be hesitant to say things that might upset the mentor, even if those things really should be voiced.

While this is a business relationship example, the same thing happens in personal relationships. Maybe your cousin is one of those people who "knows a guy" for everything. You need some repairs done around your home and you don't have a lot of money to spend. You want your cousin to refer someone to you and perhaps even "call in a favor" so you can get the job done for less money. In this case, your cousin possesses social currency and holds a degree of power.

This is why it is valuable to understand the power dynamics that exist in your relationships. Power can hamper or enable relationships as well as communication. Here are some questions to consider about power:

1. Which power currencies exist in my relationships?
2. How have power currencies affected how I communicate in my personal relationships?

3. What do I need to do to bring balance to power currencies in my relationships?

As you think about power dynamics and how they play out in your life, recognize the power currencies that exist in your relationships. Reflecting on the power currencies in your personal relationships will give you insight into how power can hamper communication. If you want to bring more balance to the power that is present in your life, you should first determine if it is, in fact, power. You do that by answering the following questions:

- Is it legitimate for this person to hold power over me?
- Does this person treat me as if they have power over me?
- What does this person have that I think I need? Do I really need it? And do I need it from this person?

Remember, power exists in a relationship because a) we allow it or submit to it, and b) there is a perceived need and a belief that the other person can serve the need.

Surely, we all come under authority. By no means am I suggesting we disrespect or disregard authority. However, we should be able to not let authority exert power over us to the point of absolute control.

Take Control of Your Communications

You now understand the seven roadblocks to communication and some strategies you can use to lessen the effect these roadblocks have on your ability to communicate with others, particularly about taboo topics. Honesty, apprehension, judgment, stigma, social influence, family dynamics, and power can have a significant impact on your life. The good news is that you only have to worry about yourself. You are not responsible for how other people behave or even what they say. Though you may be working toward a closer relationship with another person, and you just reviewed what may seem like external

73

factors that you cannot control, please remember that you are ulti-mately working on yourself. And you have total control over what you say and do.

With that in mind, we are going to delve into a key ingredient required for us to move forward on the path toward Relationship Reset: Courage.

CHAPTER 5

Develop the Courage to Communicate about the Tension

Now that you know about the seven communication roadblocks, some of which are internal and some are external, it's time to delve into the topic of courage. Courage is vital when communicating about taboo topics, because speaking your truth can be difficult. Additionally, the internal and personal work required for a Relationship Reset is not easy. But if the relationship is worth saving or worth investing in, then the work will be worth it, albeit challenging. The process may be confusing. You may even get angry and frustrated and want to give up.

You may be wondering why I am pointing out all negative aspects of what could go wrong here. I'm certainly not trying to discourage you. In fact, it's quite the opposite. I am trying to set you up for success. Often, when we embark on something new, we don't count all the costs. Yes, there are costs to a Relationship Reset. All things come with a cost. This is not a bad thing. When you understand what you are about to get into, or at least have the perspective that you may not know exactly what you are getting into, you are in a stronger position. The courage you develop now will add to that strength.

Courage, or the ability to move forward in the face of fear, grief, or anticipated pain, is exactly what we are moving toward. Usually, we are so excited about a new endeavor that we create a picture in our head of how everything is supposed to happen, complete with a fairy-tale ending. We inadvertently overlook the hard work, effort, and possible setbacks that are common. Yes, setbacks will happen. I know you want to get to the fairy-tale ending you've created in your head as quickly as possible, but remember that this is a process. As with all processes, you won't always encounter a straight line. The path may be winding. You may even feel like you are moving in a circle, rounding back to past events repeatedly with the other person. But that's okay. It's part of the process.

When things get difficult, people often want to give up, usually because they believe results should happen faster than they typically do. But if you know what is in front of you, if you go in knowing there will be challenges, you are more likely to stay the course because you understand there is not an easy or quick fix. You will have self-introspection like you've never had before. You may not like what you learn about yourself or a family member or close friend, but if you know that is what you are facing, and if you have the courage to move forward, then you are more likely to complete the journey.

The Courage to Persevere

Too many people give up on new endeavors because things don't end up how they imagined. For example, maybe you started a new diet and didn't lose 10 pounds in the first month, so you decided this diet doesn't work and you gave up. Or you got married and the two of you didn't buy a house within the first three years, so you decided you are doomed to live in an apartment forever and you gave up saving for that new home. We all have these types of thoughts, and we all make decisions based on those thoughts. The question then becomes, "How did we arrive at how something should be or how it should end?"

As you start to take ownership of your role in relationships, you may be assuming a responsibility you've never had before—a responsibility to yourself and to another person. Let's be honest here ... it is and will be difficult to initiate a conversation about taboo topics. Reflect on everything you have learned just to get into a position to even attempt such a conversation, let alone be vulnerable enough to share your truths that you uncover in the process. But there are also immense benefits to this process. On the other side of the hard work and effort, you will have a better understanding of who you are. You will learn more about yourself in a way that you have not attempted before. You will move away from talking. You will start communicating in your personal relationships. And that is a gift no one can take away.

As you move forward, you must do so with realistic expectations. Your expectations, however, should only be for yourself. You cannot hold another person to a set of expectations that you determine and that they don't know about. For example, if you were going to tell your spouse about a child given up for adoption when you were a teenager, you cannot set an expectation that they will understand, or that they will console you, or that they will attempt to aid you in searching for the child after all these years. Quite frankly, you cannot have expectations because there aren't any to have initially. Remember, you are the one choosing to address a taboo topic. You are attempting to resolve tension in the relationship that has existed for days, months, years, and in some cases even decades. You are the one who is doing the internal work to make the relationship better. You are the one taking a chance that the other person will want to do the work with you to make the relationship better. And because that is the place you are coming from, you cannot set expectations for another person and expect them to meet those expectations. It's just not realistic.

You must have courage (the mental or moral strength to venture, persevere, and withstand danger, fear, or difficulty) to move to the next steps. But before you take that step, commend yourself for getting this far. The work you have done on yourself will not be lost. You are a better person already. You have a new view of yourself now. You have a better understanding of your role in the tension within the relationship now. You have made transformative progress on yourself so far. Let's keep working.

Many factors impact your confidence in your ability to believe that you can move forward. While you may be eager to keep forging ahead and continuing the momentum you've built thus far, realize that you may encounter bumps along the road. As we learned about the seven communication roadblocks in Chapter 4, we are now going to identify possible bumps along the road to Relationship Reset. Specifically, we are going to learn about earning the right to communicate. Yes, you have to earn something here. By arming yourself with the right tools and skills, your courage will get stronger and you will be better positioned to initiate a conversation about a taboo topic.

Earn the Right to Communicate about the Taboo Subject

Having the right to communicate with someone about a particular issue is more important than most folks realize. Often, people assume because they "know you," they can broach any and every subject with you. Or, because they hold a position of authority in your life, or because they are a family member, like an aunt or sister, they can ask you anything or provide their opinion about your life. This is so not true. Why? Because we are all selective about whom we disclose information to and are vulnerable with. We don't share personal information, let alone issues that can be considered taboo, with just anyone at any time, regardless of their relation to us or relationship with us.

Whether you agree or not, you have to "earn the right" to initiate these conversations with another person. You cannot just bring up any issue with a person because you feel "I'm tired of holding it in" or "I need to get something off my chest." In fact, if that is how you feel, that is a sure sign that you are not ready to initiate the conversation. Why? Because heightened emotions are still in charge of what you are doing and what you are saying when you feel this way. You are going through this process because you don't know how to interact with the person anymore and you aren't sure how the relationship is supposed to work. This means you cannot have preconceived attitudes or expectations about how the encounter will unfold. You just don't know. The only thing you know is that you are doing the work on yourself and you are open to the process and a way forward in the relationship.

You need to consider three things when evaluating whether you have earned the right to initiate a conversation about a taboo topic: 1) length of time in the relationship; 2) degree of intimacy/closeness in the relationship; and 3) trust within the relationship. Let's look at each in detail.

Length of Time in the Relationship

How much "time in" do you have in the relationship? You need to assess how many months, years, or decades you have been in a relationship with this person. This is important because knowing someone for six months is very different from knowing someone for sixteen years. Having said that, time in a relationship does not automatically entitle you to anything. For instance, you can have a friend for ten years and still not know as much about them as someone you have known for three years. We will learn more about this in the next section when we learn about intimacy/closeness in a relationship.

There is no magic number as to how many years you must know someone in order to earn the right to start a conversation about a taboo topic, because the nature of the relationship will vary. The short answer is, "it depends." What does matter is your ability to reflect on what has happened during the time you have known them.

Quality of time compared to the quantity of time can be very different yet make all the difference with respect to relationships. Quality of the time in the relationship can be subjective. In general, you are assessing what happened during the time you've been in the relationship. What kind of things did you do over the months or years? How valuable was the time to you? Quantity is the literal amount of time. For example, if you know someone for ten years but you only talk to them two to three times a year and only see them every four years or so, that is very different from a five-year relationship where you talk every day and see each other every week.

When you think about both the quantity and quality of time, you can determine your potential credibility with another person. Overall, we all place a value on time in a relationship. The value may be positive or negative, but it is an important factor that helps us learn who someone really is, not who they pretend to be. Time gives you that.

As you think about the amount of time you have been in a relationship with the person and whether you have earned the right to approach a taboo subject with them, reflect on the following questions:

1. How does the quality of the time in the relationship compare to the quantity of time in the relationship?
2. How do I think the other person would compare the quality and quantity of time in the relationship?
3. What are the reasons why I think I have earned the right to instigate a conversation about a taboo topic with this person?

You may realize that you do not have enough quality time or quantity of time in the relationship to initiate a conversation. If that is the case, you may have great progress with some or all the remaining elements that help you earn the right to initiate a conversation about a taboo topic. If you are unsure if you have enough time in a relationship, you can always ask the other person. Yes, ask. When you approach someone with sincerity and honesty, you are being authentic. You might ask a question like, "I have something I need to talk to you about that might be a difficult conversation for both of us. But before I do that, I need to understand if the time we have invested in this relationship can withstand the conversation."

I am sure the response will be one of curiosity. First, they may want to know what exactly you want to discuss. Definitely share that with them. At that point, the other person has a choice to make. Either they will agree or disagree that you both have invested enough time in the relationship to discuss the taboo topic. Remember, you can't set expectations. More importantly, you have to respect the other person's perspective and position. You may not agree, and that's okay, but you do have to respect how they feel.

Degree of Intimacy/Closeness in the Relationship

How close are you with the other person? Closeness may seem related to "time in the relationship." While the two topics are similar, they are each unique. When we learned about time, we discussed quality versus quantity. Similar to the quality of the time spent with another person, closeness with another person can also be subjective. For example, suppose you've had a friend for seventeen years. During that time, you helped this friend bury loved ones, you let them sleep on your couch when life got hard, and you were there for the surgeries and the births of babies. You showed up, not just during the good times, but also the bad. There was the time they found out about a parent's secret child. There was also that overnight trip out of town to do something illegal. You stood ten toes down when everyone else was running away. You don't get through all the years, life events, tears, and laughter without creating a sense of reliability and dependability. In this example, seventeen years is the quantity of time. The fact that you were there to support another person during those years is the quality of time. The fact that those times occurred consistently and over a long period of time would warrant a degree of closeness. You might even say that someone who has done all those things over the years would be a best friend, or even like a brother or like a sister.

Closeness can be subjective because you may feel you are close with someone, but you really aren't. This happens because you can "know of" someone, which is very different from "knowing" someone. To "know of" someone implies you have heard the person's name before, have seen them in person out in public, or they are a friend of a friend. You really don't know the person directly. To "know" someone suggests that you have some type of relationship with them. Both are based on the degree of closeness to one another in the relationship. Realize that closeness is not dependent on who the person is. In other words, you can "know of" someone you are related to. Just because you are biologically related to another person and use the word "family" does not mean you know the person or that you are close. You can be related to a total stranger. Just because you grew up in a house with someone does not mean you are close to them. You could also live in a house full of strangers.

How intimate and/or close you are with this person matters because you are initiating a conversation about a sensitive issue, and you better know what you are talking about. Too often, people think they know the details about an issue or a person, and they don't. In reality, they probably know some of the story or heard about a part of the story. But most of the time, they form opinions about the situation, make judgments about the person, and operate as if their rendition of the story is the truth. But unless the person has told you the details directly, you don't know. And even then, you only know what the person has chosen to share with you at that time.

The point is that the greater the closeness you have with another person, the more courage you have to confront them about taboo topics. You may be concerned that you don't have an intimate or close relationship with the person. Whether you have a close relationship with the person may not be something you can gauge on your own. It could be, but it is reasonable to be unsure. The following questions will help you think through your intimacy and closeness in the relationship:

1. Would I characterize the relationship as close? If so, why? If not, why not?
2. Would the other person characterize the relationship as close? If so, why? If not, why not?
3. What do I really know about this person—either based on first-hand experience or from a conversation with the person?

After answering these questions, you may feel that you indeed have a close relationship with the person. In that case, your courage should be getting stronger. However, you may feel that you are not as close with the person as you thought, at least not close enough to initiate a conversation about a taboo topic. Much like you would ask the person if there is enough time in the relationship, you can also ask the person how close they feel the relationship really is with you. Again, with sincerity and honesty, you can say, "I have something I need to talk to you about that might be a difficult conversation for both of us. But before I do that, I need to understand if our relationship is as close as I think it is to withstand the conversation. I think our relationship is very close and here is why (elaborate on why you think you have a close relationship). What I don't know is how close you think our relationship is."

Again, you are trying to understand the other person's perspective. In earlier chapters, we discussed how perspective can be someone's reality, even if it isn't based on facts. Understanding how close each of you think the relationship is will give you the courage to initiate a conversation about a taboo topic.

Trust within the Relationship

Trust is a big deal. Most people want to be trusted by others but can find it difficult to give trust to others. Trust can be complicated. Trust represents our belief that someone will not harm us—that we are safe both in their presence and out of their presence. When you trust someone, you believe that the other person has your best interests in mind. Words like "safe," "commitment," and "harm" are connected to trust, and they are subjective. Unfortunately, there is no universal barometer for how we come to trust someone. Trust can take years to build with someone yet seconds to destroy. When trust is damaged, the relationship is damaged, and disconnection begins. We can give or withhold trust. Most people believe that if someone doesn't trust us, it's their problem. That's not necessarily true. If someone doesn't trust you, it is usually because they have experienced something with you, heard something about you, or observed behaviors from you that led them to distrust you. Just as you manage your behaviors, reputation, and words, you also manage how others trust you, to some degree.

For instance, if someone has an opinion that they do not trust people who steal, and they learn that a friend used to steal cars when they were younger, trust could come into question. Some people may feel that the past is the past and if the person hasn't stolen from them, they can be trusted. On the other hand, some people may believe that if you steal a car, you will steal money (or anything else). They believe that a thief is always a thief and can never be trusted.

Here's another example: Your cousin introduced you to a few male friends while you all were hanging out. You thought they were just friends, but they were actually there to size you up. The cousin was trying to make a deal to sell you for sex so they could pay off a debt. Would you ever trust this cousin again? Some may never trust this cousin again. Some may extend grace to a wayward soul who needs help turning their life around. There is no right answer here because we are each entitled to decide whom we deem trustworthy.

When you don't have trust in someone, you are less likely to have the courage to bring up a taboo topic with them. Therefore, you have to decide if and to what degree you trust the other person and if you think the other person has trust in you. Trust may or may not be created equal in a relationship. For example, you may trust someone to pick you up from the hospital, but you may not trust that same person to pick up your child from school and babysit until you get off work. You may trust someone enough to marry them but not trust them enough to share that you had a disabled child as a teenager who you put up for adoption after the birth. You may be wondering how someone can marry a person they do not trust completely. The short answer is, it's complicated, but it happens more often than we realize.

Several factors go into trust: character, loyalty, strength, confidence, and past behaviors, just to name a few. While it takes a great deal of time to build trust, you can lose it in seconds. The time to regain trust once lost is variable and subjective. You can lose trust in someone and still be in a relationship with them. Also realize that trust can run deeper than the context of the relationship. We often hear about "daddy issues" or "mommy issues," which are very real and can create a lot of trust issues beyond the relationship with a mother or father. In reality, many experiences can create trust issues in personal relationships that have nothing to do with parental figures at all. Psychologists often hypothesize that our family of origin holds the answers to many questions we may have in our lives as adults. Trust is one of those issues that can have a strong root in family dynamics. Remember the family roles and communication patterns from Chapter 4? Well, how you are raised and understand trust as a child greatly impacts your view and subsequent communications with others as an adult. The key here is that you have to be open about where on the trust continuum the relationship exists. Since the issue of trust is complicated, here are several questions to answer that will help you better understand your level of trust in the relationship:

1. What trust issues do I have with the other person? What trust issues does the other person have with me?
2. At what point in the relationship did the trust issues start? What caused the trust to come into question?
3. What is required for this person to gain or regain my trust? What is required for me to trust this person again?

If you don't have any trust issues in the relationship, or if you have overcome problems with trust, you are doing well. Lack of trust can pose great problems in relationships, but the good news is that you can rebuild it over time. After going through these questions, you may realize that you have some trust problems with this person or maybe they have a trust problem with you. Either way, you are likely clearer now in how you determine trustworthiness. As suggested with the other areas that strengthen courage, you can ask the person about trust in the relationship. You can say, "I trust you very much. I trust you to have my best interest at heart. I have something that I want to talk with you about. But I don't know if you trust me. If you trust that I have your best interest at heart, then I need to talk to you about something that might be a difficult conversation for both of us. Before I do that, it would be helpful to understand if we have enough trust in this relationship to withstand the conversation. Let's first talk about our trust for one another." Remember, everyone has a perspective and experiences that inform who they are and why they are the way they are. Respect their perspective.

Be a Courageous Communicator

It certainly takes courage to initiate a conversation about a taboo topic. Fortunately, you can take steps to strengthen your courage, so you can be confident in your ability to move forward. By earning the right to initiate a conversation about a taboo topic, you can move forward with a new perspective about yourself and the relationship. Now that you have examined yourself and the relationship through the lens of time, closeness, and trust, you have a realistic sense of what initiating the conversation about a taboo topic will look like for you.

All the work you have done in Chapters 1-4 gives you the foundation to find your courage. Your courage is important because you might have to make some difficult decisions in the coming days, weeks, or months as you move through this process with another person. Having done the work and having the courage is what is going to position you to have peace about those decisions. The initial stages of starting the conversation require you to establish boundaries, operate in truth, and understand commitment and accountability in a relationship, and know what to do if the conversation does not go well. You are now ready to learn about and walk through these steps to attempt the Relationship Reset.

CHAPTER 6

The Relationship Reset

Congratulations! You now have the tools you need to continue moving forward to initiate a Relationship Reset. You have done the important inner work. You can do this! Having said that, remember that you are about to bring up an issue that is the source of tension in your relationship. The other person you need to reach out to may or may not feel the tension too; and that's okay. All the work you've done to this point has been work on yourself so that you are prepared to deal with the situation, whatever the outcome or however the person does or does not choose to participate in the process. Using my Relationship Reset model, you are not making demands of the other person. This entire process is voluntary.

You may be thinking, "Well, if the person shuts me down, then that's it. I did all this work for nothing. If this is voluntary and the other person doesn't want to do it, then none of this matters." That is so not true. Perhaps the other person is just not ready to address what you want to communicate about now. No does not mean never. No simply means not now. However, I suspect that the steps you take next will open their mind and their heart to the issue, or at the very least move the relationship in a positive direction.

Here is a brief overview of how the entire process will work. We will get into specifics in a moment.

- Before you initiate the contact, you determine what you are going to communicate by identifying a specific event or time period to reference.
- Then you decide what you want to communicate.
- Next, you initiate the contact.
- Finally, you wait, listen, and then respond.

This is a cyclical process (see figure below). After you wait, listen, and then respond, you can go back to determining what to communicate. In real-world application, I understand that all will not move through each step, in order, or perfectly. I have provided guidance and steps to assist you in moving through the process. While you may move through the steps in any order, it is important to know the steps and go back to each one.

Because this is a cyclical process, you may find yourself moving through this process repeatedly. Each time you want to initiate communication about a new issue that has not been resolved, you can employ these steps. When you use this process, the conversation won't feel like an attack on the other person. In fact, each time you go through these steps you are strengthening the relationship. Your relationship will grow to a level that has not existed before.

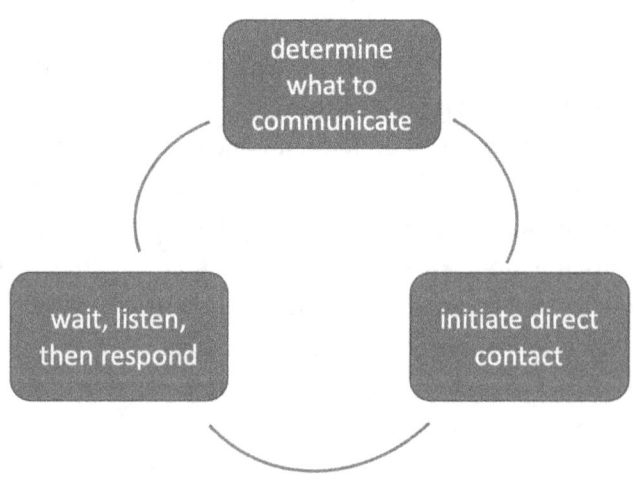

Step 1: Determine What to Communicate

Real-Life Application

Now we are going to walk through a real-life scenario from one of my coaching clients. This will help you see a real-world example of how to apply the skills you have learned. My client, Alexis (not her real name), has a mother who has suffered with the disease of addiction for many years. The addiction caused great turmoil, pain, and estrangement between them. The mom was released from prison and Alexis wanted to try to reconnect. To begin, I led her through the inner work. Alexis developed a communication mindset and identified the communication roadblocks that could affect the Relationship Reset process. Specifically, we worked on judgments made about drug addiction and being a convicted felon. We also worked through identifying the family communication patterns and family roles. Alexis is now at the phase of making contact and initiating the reset with her mother. Before she made the phone call, I prepped Alexis by letting her know that her mother may or may not answer the call. Either way, Alexis was prepared with what to say. I coached her through both scenarios. In the case that her mom answers the call, I asked her to communicate with me exactly what she wanted her mother to know and do.

Communicating how the relationship has impacted life and affected communication is so important at this stage. This is part of the "why" behind the "what." In Chapter 2, I discussed that oftentimes we make decisions in relationships based on the "what" of a thing and not the "why" of a thing. By communicating what we want the other person to know, we are expressing our feelings and lived experience of the relationship as well as vulnerabilities.

Here is how Alexis responded:

"I want my mom to know that I want to correct some of the wrongs of the past. I want her to know that I made mistakes in this relationship. She needs to know that I think she made mistakes too. I have to tell her that I am still very hurt by the drug addiction and dealing with the revolving prison door that seems to afflict her life like a plague. I want her to know that I have been working on myself and I want to make a real effort to reset our relationship. I want her to know that I am scared that this may work, or it may not work. Both outcomes scare me because I don't know what having a normal relationship with her will be like and I don't know what will happen if we aren't able to come together on this. I want her to know that I am open to getting my mom back. I want her to know that even though I am an adult and I had to grow up without her, it doesn't mean I don't need my mom in my life. It doesn't mean my kids don't need their grandmother. I want to share that it has taken me a long time to get to this point with myself. I want to share that I believe that I am ready to work on this relationship."

Being able to communicate what you expect of another person is essential because it allows space for revelation and discussion around expectations. Anger and resentment are often rooted in unmet expectations. Unfortunately, expectations are often misguided, formed without all the facts, and may not be communicated with the other person, ultimately leading to disappointment. In short, disappointment occurs when expectations are not met.

With that said, the questions to ask yourself are: "What is the expectation? Is this the right expectation? How did I arrive at this expectation? Does the person know I expect them to do this?" Too often, people confuse expectations with wishing. Therefore, you need to make sure your expectations are based on facts of the situation and not what you wish the other person would do or become. You cannot hold people to account for your dream or "idea" of them or who you wish they were. Equally, you cannot hold people to unrealistic and unknown expectations. For example, it is unrealistic to expect someone who does not have a college degree or experience in engineering to get a job as an engineer just because they have expressed interest in the field. However, it is realistic to expect the person to identify a path toward becoming an engineer with clear steps of how to get there. It is even more important to communicate your thoughts and expectations so there is an understanding.

Communicating expectations allows you to check-in with the other person, and if necessary, adjust misguided expectations. Therefore, think about what you want the other person to do. What is the ask? For Alexis, she said:

"I want my mom to put forth the effort to be in a relationship with me. Whatever that may look like, I expect an honest effort. No bullshit this time. No more lies. No secrets. No more feeling sorry for yourself. No more blaming everyone else for what has happened. Just straight up effort. Even if there are setbacks, I need effort this time. No more just waiting to see what will happen. This time has to be on purpose."

No matter the situation, you can communicate what you want and why. Only you know what you are willing to give to this relationship. Only you know the reason behind what you are saying, why you are saying it, and the intended action or outcome from the interaction. Now, it's time to insert what you want to communicate in a way that is safe for you.

Even though there is risk in this process, you need to ensure that there is respect, comfort, and safety for yourself. To do that, you have to establish boundaries.

Establishing Boundaries

Drs. Henry Cloud and John Townsend have done wonderful work explaining boundaries. In their many books on the topic, they explain in simple language what boundaries are and why we should have them. Thanks to them, boundaries are now commonly understood concepts. As they explain, boundaries help you to be clear about what you are for and against and what you will and won't tolerate in relationships. We form boundaries with words and actions.

So, why do so many of us still have trouble with boundaries? What is it about boundaries that makes us uncomfortable? What is the fear? Is it past experiences? Maybe. Typically, we fear how we think others will respond once we set some boundaries. There it is again: "Think." We cannot possibly know what will happen, yet we decide about setting boundaries or adjusting them based on fear. Sometimes we simply give up altogether because we feel people are not honoring our boundaries.

Establishing boundaries, respecting them, and not crossing them is essential if you want to have healthy relationships and live your life authentically. Boundaries allow you to limit or at the very least consciously manage the stress and strain that can cause havoc on your mental wellbeing. Establishing and then communicating boundaries allows you to identify what makes you comfortable or uncomfortable. The key here is to not just establish the boundaries, but to also communicate them so others know what they are. You cannot simply assume others will know what your boundaries are. This is also true when attempting to reset a relationship. You have to allow for both parties to establish a stake in the relationship and agree on boundaries and expectations moving forward. You decide what you will and will not do together (through communication) in the relationship.

The first step to determining what boundaries make sense for you is to list your personal values. Values can have many definitions and interpretations. There isn't a right or wrong answer here. When it comes to personal values, there's no "one size fits all" approach. Values are different for each of us. Therefore, in this context, I define personal values as characteristics we identify as being part of the moral code that guides our actions and defines who we are. They are what we consider important, the things that matter to our wellbeing and happiness.

When setting boundaries, identifying and communicating personal values allows us to have a better understanding of who we are and what matters to us most. Setting boundaries that are aligned with personal values creates legitimacy and truthfulness to who we are to ourselves and to others. When there is a link between boundaries and values, our communication with the other person is genuine.

I walked Alexis through the value identification process. Following are the personal values Alexis felt were important:

Spirituality	Strength	Peace
Honesty	Family	Faith
Respect	Integrity	Compassion
Kindness	Love	Diversity
Dependability	Self-respect	Loyalty
Safety	Justice	Forgiveness

This is a great exercise for you to do too. Write down your personal values. After creating your list of values, consider this question: "When reconnecting with the other person, what is important for me to have emotional and mental space as well as physical space to feel safe?" Since this is a big question, we can break it down into two parts. First, focus on the emotional/mental aspect. What do you need to feel safe with the other person on an emotional/mental level? Think about what you need to be able to express yourself to another person who you believe cares about your own emotional experience. Emotional safety is important to the communication process because when our body and mind experience safety, we can listen, empathize, and connect better.

Here is what Alexis needed for emotional/mental safety:

"I know that I need to not feel taken advantage of; not feel used; not feel disregarded; that my opinions matter; that I will not be put in danger by another person; that my beliefs matter; and that I am not unfairly and unknowingly judged. I don't want to feel bullied."

Once you've identified the emotional/mental aspects, move on to the physical aspects of safety. Physical safety may seem like something that should be considered standard; it's given. Well, that may not always be the case for everybody. It is important to be in a physical space where you feel protected from harm or injury. Therefore, consider what you need to be physically safe. Consider such things as locations, items in those locations, people, etc. This is basically about anything in the physical world that would impact your emotional wellbeing.

Alexis' response was:

"Since I was molested as a child, I cannot be around people that rape, molest, or sexually assault people. I am even uncomfortable around strippers. Social workers scare me. I do not like being around guns. I am uncomfortable in an environment where there isn't any structure, like no rules at all, and everybody just does whatever they want. Oh, I am also uncomfortable when I am in a house full of strangers."

Armed with both personal values and needs for emotional/mental and physical safety, it's time to start building boundaries. You will build a boundary in the way that we worked through the exercise. It's a relatively simple equation:

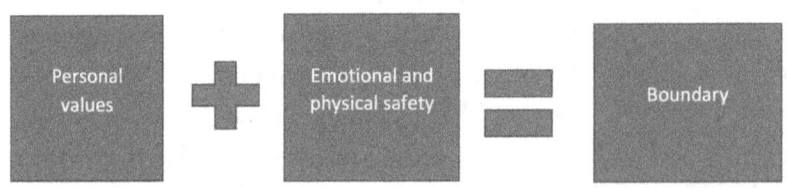

Now, I will apply the equation to an example so you can see how this works in the real-world. Alexis identified several of these factors, so we'll use them:

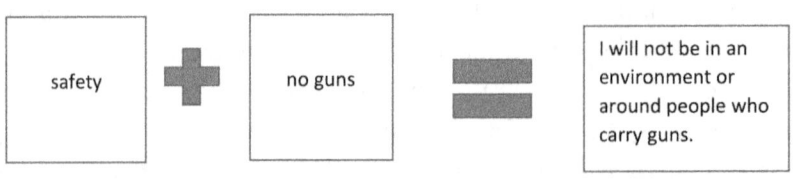

While I included a practical example for how to create boundaries using what Alexis was able to come up with, it makes sense for me to also provide an example that uses more abstract personal values so you can try this for yourself. The example below considers:

Self-respect + No abuse = I will not allow anyone to abuse me in any way. That includes verbal, emotional, sexual, and physical abuse.

Back to Alexis. The next step for Alexis was to create boundaries in the relationship with her mom based on this exercise. Alexis, came up with these boundaries:

"I think a good boundary might be that I will only meet in public places, at least for now. Another one might be, I will not have Mom meet my children right now. Also, I will not purchase drugs, liquor, or cigarettes for my mom. I will attend AA or NA meetings with her if she asks. I will not give Mom money; if she needs money for a true need, like rent, I will pay the company directly, if I choose to."

After you have several boundaries, you can move to communicating the boundaries. Remember, it is only when you communicate your boundaries that the other person is responsible for respecting the boundary and can be held accountable when disrespecting the boundary.

I asked Alexis to imagine how she would communicate her boundaries to her mother. Her response was:

"If I am going to give all my effort to make this work, I need to feel safe. So, there are some boundaries I need to establish for me to keep working on this relationship with you. I will only meet in public places, at least for now. I will not allow you to meet my children right now. I will not purchase drugs, liquor, or cigarettes for you. I will attend AA or NA meetings with you if you want me to. I will not give you money directly; however, if you need money for a true need, like rent, I will pay the company directly."

When you establish boundaries, it is valuable to delve into how the past has shaped your communication. Often, you cannot move into the present without revisiting the past. Addressing the past history of the relationship and having a mutual understanding and respect (while not necessarily agreement), is particularly important at this stage.

The Past

An immense problem with the past is that everybody wants to revisit it, and some can be held hostage to it. When discussing it, most folks do not put parameters around it. For them, "the past" means all the previous years leading up to the very moment in question. Dealing with the past can be a massive undertaking because the memories and feelings can go so far back in time and can be mired with bias, errors, and misremembering.

Unfortunately, unresolved issues from the past continue to show up in our life and come out of our mouth in different ways. We have spent so much time going through the work that we are doing on ourselves because we have to live with ourselves. The deep thoughts in your mind and the voices in your head never leave you. People come and go, but you are always your own reflection. Addressing the past by identifying and communicating your feelings that are born from past hurts, shame, and guilt is a gift that allows you to experience a sense of freedom in the relationship that you may not have had with this person before.

If you are going to move back in time, you need to identify time periods or a specific incident to be addressed. Why? It can be overwhelming for the person on the receiving end of your message to be subjected to years of memories that can span all or part of your life. I think we can all agree that this approach usually doesn't work. Further, it often puts both parties in a defensive communication position, essentially closing the communication process. So, it makes sense to provide background and parameters to the information from the past that you are sharing. Also, establishing parameters gives the other person a starting point for where, when, and how the feelings started that caused the strain in the relationship.

Successful communication occurs when everyone has space to be brutally honest without opinions or interruptions. That happens when you give someone that foundation from which you are speaking. There is power in standing in your truth about what you will discuss, what you will not discuss, and why. To establish this, answer these questions about the situation or event you are going to talk about: 1) When did it happen? 2) How do you remember it happened? 3) How did it affect you? And 4) Why has the tension (or anger or resentment, etc.) gone on for so long?

I asked Alexis these four questions and her response was:

"I think we really stopped communicating when I was about 13 years old. Up until that point, I only saw my mom every few years. We never lived in the same house. She came to visit sometimes. Our relationship was always awkward to me because my mom would come and visit me and not live with me. We seldom went anywhere together. So as a child, I was just confused. Nobody ever explained the situation. I did not understand how my family worked, really. When she did visit, we would talk a little but because I was a child, the conversation was mostly about school and sports. As I got older the visits became less and less. Then I realized my mom was in prison. I found out by accident because I overheard a conversation about my mom getting 'busted' and 'sent upstate.' Because of the prison time, I started getting letters from her. But again, nobody told me what was really going on. I wrote a few letters back but because I felt lied to, left out, and invisible, I stopped writing. It was at that point that I feel the communication stopped. My entire life has been affected by her drug addiction and prison time. Because I was never really told what happened, I made up my own stories. Because of the lack of honesty within my family, I do not trust many people. I did not have a safe and secure foundation growing up and I was unstable for many years. I fear addiction so I have never smoked anything, taken a drink, or experimented with drugs. My life has focused on not becoming her. The anger has gone on for so long because I have never had the opportunity to confront my mom and tell her my version of what happened and what I had to endure without her there."

Finding the words and then communicating them to the other person strengthens your courage to continue with the process. With this foundation laid, it's time to make contact.

Step 2: Initiate Direct Contact

You have several options when it comes to contacting someone. You can call, mail a letter, contact via social media, send a text, or send an email. The important thing is that you initiate contact directly. That means do not go through a friend or a third party to do this. The communication must come from you. There are benefits to all these mediums of contact.

- Call: Calling is a gamble. Phone numbers change. They may answer; they may not. And we don't know why they may or may not answer. The benefit here is that you made an attempt. I will add that if you make a call, you need a plan in place for either outcome. It may be helpful to write out what you want to say, as we just discussed. Similarly, if they don't answer, think about what you are going to do next. Will you leave a message? Do you make another call? If so, when? If not, then will you try another mode of contact?
- Mail a personal letter: You may think that mailing a letter is outdated. I assure you that people read mail and they definitely read personal letters. Does this mean there is a 100% guarantee your recipient will read your letter? Not necessarily. However, there is a high probability that they will. The benefit of a letter is that you can put it all on paper. Now, when I say "all" I do not mean "all of the past." Remember, you have to focus on a particular event. Consider your feelings about the situation and how it has

impacted your life since it started. Why make contact now? What do you want to express?

- Social media: The onset of social media has created a very unfiltered and uncontrolled way to bestow unsolicited opinions about anything and everything to the world. In this case, you are attempting to make direct contact about a personal issue, so my suggestion is to make the contact as private as possible. Do not blast all their "followers" and "friends" with this. Instead, send a brief message that tells them a) why you are reaching out, and b) what you are going to do next to make contact. This looks like the following: "Hello [name], this is [name]. I know it has been [time period] since we last connected, which is why I am reaching out to you now. Social media can be so impersonal, but I wanted to reach you this way to let you know that I will be mailing you a letter [or insert medium of communication] that gives more detail about why I am contacting you now. I hope that you will read it [or answer the call]."

- Text: Handle a text in the same manner as a message via social media. Keep it short and specific.

- Email: Email is not exactly like mailing a letter, but it has many similar characteristics. You may think email is an outdated medium that is rarely used, except when at work. Well, from a business perspective, the number one way to garner interest, feedback, and gain new customers is through email. No, you are not trying to sell a widget here. But you are trying to get the attention of someone. I provide the business example so you understand that sending an email works. Because an email is being sent to one person, you have some assurance of privacy. With that said, you will follow a similar format to sending a social media message. This looks like the following: "Hello [name], this is [name]. It may seem like I'm contacting you out of the blue. It has been a while since we last connected, which is why I am reaching out to you now. The way things have been between us has not settled well with me. I have acted badly towards you, and I feel you have acted badly towards me in some ways as well. I wanted to reach you this way to let you know that I have been working on myself, and I know that our relationship is one that I want to start over. I hope you will reply but understand if you don't. Know that I am open to connecting with you whenever you are ready."

Understand that you may not get a response immediately or at all; that is okay. While you can hope for a reconciliation, the other person may not be receptive.

Alexis decided to make contact by calling her mom. Surprisingly, her mom answered the call and Alexis was able to read through all the work we had done. Specifically, Alexis shared what she wanted her mom to know, expectations, boundaries, and feelings about the past. Her mom initially cried but expressed relief that Alexis reached out. At this point, Alexis and her mother are working on their communication in their relationship and are moving in the right direction.

Step 3: Wait, Listen, and Then Respond

While Alexis was able to get immediate feedback from her mom, you may not be as lucky. In some cases, the response may be fast, or you may be waiting for a while. You may get no response at all. But if there is a response, it is important to listen. Give the other person an opportunity to share their feelings and position on the situation as well. During that time, you are not talking. You are listening.

Listening is a key skill you need to activate during this relationship process. Listening does not mean you focus on determining when to cut the person off to make your point. Listening does not mean you focus on one part of what they said and prepare a defense while the person is still talking. On the contrary, *listening means that you are intentionally available to the lived experience and feelings of the other person.* You are silent. This is not a time to redirect the conversation back to your experiences. While the experiences are connected, you will find great value in receiving the other person's perspective. Granted, this can be a dangerous moment primarily because you may not agree with the recollection of events, or you may want to defend yourself if you feel you are being attacked. So keep this in mind: When you initiated the contact, you communicated your experience and feelings, and now you are allowing space for the other person to do the same.

When responding to the person, remember that you are reacting to the feelings and experiences of the other person. This is not a time to focus on the accuracy of facts or making judgments. Be curious about what the other person said, which means you are asking questions for understanding. A good way to determine if you understand something that was said is to repeat it back using your own words and your interpretation. For example, you can say, "When you said XX, did you mean YY?" Or "When you said XX, I understood it to mean YY. Is that right?" You may discover that your interpretation of what was said is totally off base with what was meant. At that point, you can ask, "Can you help me understand what you meant when you said XX?" Checking for understanding will alleviate much confusion and stress.

A Word of Caution Before Initiating Your Relationship Reset

Many people are excited about going through this process. But before you do, remember that the outcome may not be as positive as Alexis's was. In fact, the relationship could end up in worse condition than when you started. I applaud you for your efforts in attempting to reset the relationship with another person; however, they may not be ready to communicate about the issue you want to bring to the forefront. It's also possible that you start with sStep 1 and the entire situation goes off the rails. Despite efforts to genuinely share your experience and feelings about the taboo topic, the person may become so angry, frustrated, or defensive that everything stops. They may hang up the phone. They may storm off or leave the location. A lot of outcomes are possible here, but you will be able to respond in such a way that there is space for reconciliation in the future. Here's how:

- *Identify what happened*: While this is your perception of events, it is significant to process your own understanding of what occurred.
- *What role did each person play in the outcome:* Deciding who did what and who said what can quickly explode into blame, particularly since you have not addressed the taboo topic, which might add additional "baggage" to the explosion of events. This is not about blame. Identifying roles allows you to own your part in what happened and identify the part you think the other person played in what happened. This is important because one person is not exclusively responsible for a breakdown in communication. This is about accountability and being able to have an answer for the question, "How did we get here?"
- *What needs to happen next:* The reality is that you may not know what needs to happen next exactly. But you do know that the initial attempt did not go well. And that's okay. You can move through the steps again, except the core of what you say may sound more like: "The last time I reached out to you, it did not go well. I accept responsibility for my part in what happened. Specifically, I know that I did (state your role). I still would like to reset our relationship and address XX issue, but before we even do that, we should start with what led to our breakdown."
- *Moving forward:* The next steps on how to move forward may not be as clear as you would like them to be. Since this is a communicative process, you should decide your next steps alone. The other person also has a responsibility to re-engage. However, you cannot make anybody do anything. You can only control and manage your own actions. You

102

can go back to the steps and add what you would like to happen to the previous statement. That might sound something like: "The last time I reached out to you, it did not go well. I accept responsibility for my part in what happened. Specifically, I know that I did (state your role). I still would like to reset our relationship and address XX issue, but before we even do that, we should start with what led to our breakdown. In order to do that, I admit that I did XXX, which seemed to make you angry. I thought you were angry because you hung up the phone on me and did not answer when I called you back five times. I do not want us to get to that place again. Can you share what it was about our last encounter that led to the blow up?"

When you approach the situation in this manner, you create space and opportunity for honest communication. Further, you are moving from accusation and judgment to recognizing that your perception of what happened may not be how the other person perceived what happened. Despite how situations may turn out, the outcome does not have to be final. Remember, always leave the light on and the door open for the person to feel welcome to enter your life when they are ready to do so. They may not immediately come back. This could take months, years, or not happen at all. The important thing is the inner peace you get knowing you did what you could to forge a relationship with the person. That is all that you can do. And for that, you should be proud of yourself—not for what you did to connect with the other person but for the work you did on yourself in the process of managing the relationship.

What to Do When You Can't Connect

While we were able to move through a scenario with Alexis in which both people were able to connect with one another, that is not always the case for everyone. There are situations, like estrangement, abandonment, and even death, that affect our ability to make contact or to close the communication loop about the unresolved issues. Let's take a look at these issues.

In personal relationships, whether it's between family members or close friends, estrangement occurs. Estrangement is often defined as intentionally distancing oneself from another, both physically and emotionally, to deal with unresolved issues. Estrangement is different from having a fight or conflict with someone because usually in those instances, there is some continuance of the relationship despite the tension that is present. Here we are talking about complete dissolution of the relationship. Many of us find ourselves in this situation whether we instigated the estrangement, or the other person estranged themselves from us. In his book *Fault Lines*, Karl Pillemer shares findings from breakthrough research on estrangement. He found that 1 in 4 U.S. adults have become estranged from their families. This is not a small problem. This is a societal epidemic. Estrangement can have many causes, including issues from the past, unmet expectations, and even the residue of divorce.

Here's the real deal, and I have mentioned this before: we cannot make anybody do anything. In the matter of estrangement, that advice does not change. You have to focus on what you do. You can only control your actions, so that's what you need to do.

Often, estrangement occurs because of hurt feelings. There might be a sense of "being wronged" in some way. You may be wondering about forgiveness in this situation. Sure, there is a place for that, but remember, you are focused on yourself. Just like you cannot make anybody do anything, you also cannot make anybody forgive. Further, forgiveness is not created equal. What one may consider forgiveness another may not. While the topic of forgiveness is beyond the scope of this book, we are going to examine the best way forward when you find yourself estranged from another.

Estrangement can be an interesting space because you can either know or not know why you are estranged from another person. With that said, you can take certain actions if you wish to reconcile with the person. Regardless of whether you know the reason for the estrangement or whether you played a part in it, the steps to initiate a Relationship Reset are similar. Focus on what you know, not what you think you know. In this case, the only thing you know is that there is an estrangement, and you probably know the approximate timeline of when it started. Unless the other person told you the specific reason why you don't know much else. Even if you did learn a reason at some point, over time reasons change, and people change. So, you cannot hold onto a reason whether it was stated or you are making assumptions. Neither is helpful here.

Like estrangement, abandonment can be an equally traumatic situation that you may find yourself in. Abandonment is when you feel you have been physically or emotionally "left" by someone. This feeling can differ from estrangement in that you can still be in the presence of the person who you feel abandoned you. Yes, you can still talk to this person and feel abandoned by them. This is very plausible. Think about a parent who remarries after a divorce and a child who feels that the parent chose the new spouse over them. How about a child who was left on the church steps and later adopted? Both situations can cause abandonment issues and not surprisingly can lead to estrangement in the relationship. Like the estrangement situation, both parties may not agree on whether abandonment occurred, particularly if there is still contact with the person. It could be that the person feels they did not abandon you. Remember, this is not about being right; this is about communicated feelings and lived experiences for understanding. Misunderstandings or imperfect recall is to be expected; that is the point of communicating—to gain understanding.

Finally, the other person may not be available to communicate with due to death or the presence of a disease that affects cognitive abilities. Regardless of why you cannot have this conversation with the other person—whether it's due to estrangement, abandonment, or death—you can still close the communication loop.

When the other person is not available, you may feel like you will not be able to move past the pain because the other person will never know what they did. My question is, "How do you know that?" Quite simply, you don't. Just because you did not witness the person experiencing pain or "having to pay" or "having to answer" for what they did or said does not mean they didn't suffer with inner demons because of their actions. Just because someone is not available to move through this process with you directly does not mean they are "getting away with it." Further, I have mentioned earlier in the book that the focus is not to get back at the other person or to "set them straight." Rather, you are moving through a process to create peace, healing, and resolve for yourself about unresolved matters and taboo events that have occurred in your relationships.

When resolving an issue with someone you cannot connect with, you move through the cyclical process we just learned about, except you only have two steps instead of three. The two steps you have are: 1) determine what to communicate, and 2) initiate contact.

You still need to determine what to communicate. In this case, you can't make direct contact because the person is not available, but you can choose a medium to communicate your feelings and lived experience. There are several ways you can attempt to contact the person. You can visit their resting place (if they are deceased), write a letter, or share your feelings and lived experiences with a trusted loved one. There are benefits to all these mediums of contact.

- Visiting their resting place: Physically going to a cemetery, mausoleum, or burial site creates a sense of confronting the person. Of course, they are not there in person; however, seeing a headstone or visiting an urn allows you to come face-to-face with a symbol of the person, making it seem real. You can write and then read what you want to communicate, or you can simply speak from memory. Since the person can't respond, it's okay to freestyle a bit.

- Write a letter: Writing is a great way to express yourself in an authentic way. The action of physically writing out your emotions is valuable because it gives you a new perspective. It allows you to take all that you've been holding inside and become an observer to the emotions, giving you clarity and peace. Granted, you can't mail a letter to this person if they are deceased or you have no way to make contact due to estrangement, but you can write the letter and read it aloud. Simply find a private space and freely read the letter. You can express emotions (cry, scream, shout, etc.) to get it all out. After you read the letter, burn it. There is something healing about fire consuming paper and creating ashes that symbolizes complete destruction. In that way, the unresolved issue has been closed.
- Share your feelings with a trusted loved one: After you write your letter to the person, you can read it aloud to someone you trust. The person you choose to read the letter to needs to understand that this is strictly a listening party —they are not to speak. They are there to be an unbiased, non-judgmental ear to whatever you want to say. You may want to discuss the issue with your confidant afterwards or not. This is your opportunity to express yourself however you like. Afterwards, you can also burn the letter together.

A New Beginning

As you can see, a Relationship Reset isn't easy. You may encounter bumps along the road. But the road is forgiving and will be a bit easier to travel the more you use it. Now that you have invested the time to discover who you are and who you are becoming, you should have the courage to initiate a conversation about a taboo topic. You should also be able to appreciate your feelings and lived experience in the relationship with another person and communicate that authentically.

Again, this is a process that you move through with people you are close to and those you care about and love. I mention that because one of the main ingredients to this process is that you must care enough, and you must love enough, to do it.

Think about the relationship you want to reset. Do you care enough to do the reset? Do you love enough to do the reset?

So, what's stopping you?

It's time to do it.

CHAPTER 7

When It's Time to Walk Away

When you think of ending a relationship, your first thought is likely that of a romantic break-up or divorce. But relational endings are not exclusive to a marital or dating relationship. The fact is that certain people or relationships in general may no longer be healthy or viable to your overall well being. And if that's the case, you may need to make the tough decision to end the relationship. However, this is not about labeling someone or the relationship as "bad." Rather, it is about grasping the notion that you can manage who has access to you. By access, I mean allowing other people and things to use your time, thoughts, resources, etc. This becomes particularly difficult if you still must see the person or be around them. Think about a brother you no longer talk to … or the parent you wish to never see again. These are not ideal situations, but they do happen. Recent research led by Sarah Schoppe-Sullivan reveals that more than 50% of mothers are estranged from and haven't communicated with an adult child in over a year. There are many explanations for this, ranging from struggles with mental illness, family members turning the child against the parent, prior abuse, and personality clashes. Over the life course of any relationship, there will be seasons and circumstances when you stop communicating with someone. Sometimes you may reunite, while other times you don't. This is also true for family members.

Remember, just because you are related to someone does not mean you have to be "in a relationship" with them. My goal is for you to feel empowered to take inventory of your relationships, and if any of them are not serving you or the other person well, have the courage to decide whether it makes sense to end it. Let's just be honest … ending a relationship is not easy. Making the decision to end a relationship can be daunting. After all, we could be talking about many years of friendship and memories. If it is a relative, you may be wondering,

"What will it be like at the family reunion?" That's fair. Sometimes you may feel like it is easier to at least keep up the facade of a relationship rather than to deal with the aftermath of ending it. But answer this: "What is your peace worth to you?" Or better yet, "How valuable is having a sound mind?"

If your answers to those questions make you realize that someone in your life is jeopardizing your peace of sound mind, then you probably just want to know what to do. There are telltale signs that it may be time to end a relationship. For example, perhaps you dread getting a phone call from or seeing a certain person in public. Or maybe you find yourself saying no more often than yes to invitations. If staying in a relationship causes consistent pain—physically, emotionally, verbally—it may be time to end it. If you have to become a different person in order to be in the relationship or tolerate behavior or comments that violate your values system or are abusive, it may be time to end it. The ending doesn't have to be this big production or conclude with the police getting called or explosive drama; but sometimes that does happen. The bottom line is that you are responsible for taking care of you. You cannot take care of others if you are unwell.

In this chapter we are going to walk through what to consider when ending a relationship. Surprisingly, before you end a relationship, you also need to consider your commitment to the relationship. I know, it seems counterintuitive; how can you plan to end a relationship yet still decide if you are committed or not? Level of commitment gives great insight into how you really view the relationship. When you think about it, commitment exists on a continuum. It can also vary based on the relationship. But if you are going to put forth effort and do the work, then you should do *all* the work. By that I mean you should determine your level of commitment. Remember, I mentioned this is a continuum, so what you discover today is not necessarily static. As situations and circumstances change, so can your level of commitment.

Commitment to the Relationship

Determining your level of commitment in a relationship may seem unnecessary, but I guarantee it provides a clear understanding for you about where this person ranks in your life. I know, you may not want to think about ranking your friends or family members, but you do it naturally anyway. Think about the time your cousin asked you to come with them to meet their child whom they did not know they had for the very first time. They asked you because it was awkward and scary, and they wanted your support. Because of the strength of your friendship, kinship, and your commitment to maintaining the relationship, you went. Comparatively, when your mother asked you to go with her to the attorney's office to sign divorce papers, you said no. What is the difference between the two situations? Why does one person get a yes and another person get a no? Think back to Chapter 4, when we discussed the length of the relationship and the amount of quality time invested. All of that comes into play here. We are willing to do some things for people that we aren't willing to do for others. That is your starting point.

Think back over your relationships and answer the following questions:

Who am I in a relationship with that I am less committed to?

1. What have I been willing to do (and not do) in the relationship for the person?
2. What specific reasons did I do (or not do) those things?
3. Do I want to do more for this person and the relationship?

Who am I in a relationship with that I feel is less committed to me?

1. Why do I feel that the person is less committed to me?
2. How has this person shown up for me (or not) in the relationship?
3. Do I want commitment from this person? If so, why? If not, why not?

Your answers to these questions will help you evaluate your level of commitment to the relationship. From your perspective, you may decide that you are committed, and you think the other person is committed as well. Knowing that you are committed to the relationship helps you understand whether you should end the relationship. If you answered positively, it makes sense to attempt to maintain the relationship.

If you feel the relationship is not where you want it to be or isn't all that it could be, you can recommit. Recommitment is coming to the realization that you want to do better. That means not just saying you want to be better in the relationship, but actually doing what is necessary for the relationship to be better. The "doing" part are the steps we learned about in Chapter 6. You would simply go through those steps to recommit to the relationship.

Comparatively, if you answered these questions and realized the relationship lacks commitment, you might consider evaluating the relationship and possibly identifying if it makes sense to end it or if you want to recommit to the relationship. Sometimes, we casually drop some relationships, whether intentional or unintentional. If the lack of commitment is a result of competing demands (caretaker for parents) or changes in life (new baby) and you want to recommit, you can go through the steps in Chapter 6. It's important to recognize that in relationships there is a degree of responsibility, and you should know if you can or cannot meet the responsibility.

Relational responsibility (or relational accountability) allows us to identify what we will and will not do in the relationship. It also indicates what we are willing to be called-out on if we aren't following through; it goes hand-in-hand with commitment.

Every person has a part to play and is accountable for their role in a relationship. This means you can be held accountable to yourself as well as to others in the relationship. Lack of accountability weakens the commitment. But for accountability to be known, you must communicate it. Just as you communicate expectations to others, you also have to communicate responsibility. You are moving to a space where you are giving another person permission to "check you" on your stuff. If you are truly serious about making a change, you need safeguards in place to keep yourself on track. The people you trust to be safeguards are just that—safe people. These are trusted confidants that understand your goals and what you are trying to do; they are not people who will sabotage or judge you if you fall short. They are accountability partners. The accountability they offer is more from a space of encouragement and reinforcement. They help ensure that your actions are in alignment with your goals. Realize that change occurs through consistency. Many of us are not experts at being self-regulated, so having an accountability partner is a surefire way to keep consistently moving toward your goal.

Time to Say Goodbye

If, after thoughtful consideration and possibly even input from your accountability partner and sessions with a counselor or therapist, you decide that the relationship is simply not what you need it to be or you just can't give what's required to manage the relationship, then walking away is an option. Ending a relationship does not have to be perceived as winning or losing. It's just a change in the season of the relationship. It just is.

You can follow a process to uncommit. And yes, it does mean you are communicating that to the other person. You may think that it's easier to just "leave them on red." After all, why can't you just stop calling and texting? After a while, they will take the hint, right? While I'm sure it seems easier to fade out of someone's life, the purpose of the work we are doing in this book is to not only be clear and effective in our communication but also to be better in how we manage ourselves and others whom we are in relationship with.

With that said, it is perfectly acceptable to have a conversation with your brother about stopping contact. Why does that seem so hard to do? Maybe you think the other person does not want to stop communication. You may even think, "We're family. We are supposed to talk to each other." But are we though? If a relationship causes strife, pain, and anxiety, and if you can't find a way to come to a resolution, why continue exposing yourself to that? Why is walking away not an option? The origin of the relationship should not be prioritized over personal health and wellbeing.

Often, whether a relationship is with a family member or friend, both people feel any strain that exists. Do not assume that the other person will fight to stay in the relationship. While that may happen, chances are the other person has feelings similar to yours. You can go back to the steps you learned in Chapter 6 and apply those here. To refresh your memory, here are the steps. Step 1: determine what to communicate; Step 2: initiate direct contact; Step 3: wait, listen, and then respond. Using this framework, you decide that you are going to communicate that you no longer want to have a friendship with this person. You contact them. Then you wait, listen, and respond. While the words printed on this page are easy to read, following through with the action steps may be more difficult. I get that. You are more anxious or even fearful about the thought of telling someone you don't want to communicate with them anymore than you are about staying in contact with them. That is a normal reaction.

I'm sure an example of what this looks like will help. Let's see how this situation can play out in real life.

Suppose you need to tell a family member that you cannot continue to communicate with them. Revisit the steps. What are you going to communicate? In this instance, you know you want to communicate that you can no longer engage in a relationship with them. How are you going to communicate it? Next, you decide how you want to contact them (text, call, social media, letter). When you make contact, it is important to state why you want to talk. For example, "I have been thinking about our relationship, and I want to share my thoughts with you." You might then say, "We have spent a lot of time together over the years and have done a lot together. Some of it good and some of it bad. Lately, I have been evaluating where I am in my life and how I need to move forward. I have thought a lot about our relationship, and the truth is, I have a lot of pain and anxiety around it. When you called CPS on me because you thought I wasn't a good mother, that hurt me. While I kept my kids because the charges were unfounded, my life was a mess for quite a while because of what you did. I will no longer subject myself to ongoing derogatory comments from you about how I dress or where I work. Your judgments and unsolicited comments pierce me like daggers. I have to stop communication with you. At this point, every time you call, or I see you at grandma's house, I dread what might happen or what you might say to me around other family members. It is embarrassing. It is degrading. I'm done with it. I will not keep doing this. The only solution that I have at this point is to stop regular communication with you. It might be weird when we see each other at family events or run into each other at the grocery store, but I will be cordial with you. I have no problem speaking to you or saying hi. I just will not have an ongoing relationship with you. Regular contact with you is too painful for me. In fact, it has resulted in me fighting to keep my kids. I feel that it is not safe for me to continue to be in a relationship with you. This is not to say that this is forever, but it is at least for right now, I have to stop communicating with you. I ask that you give me the space to do that."

It is important to use "I" statements. This is not about blame or judgment. You are making the decision and taking action, so frame everything as an "I" statement; otherwise, you'll come across as blaming the other person. The final next step is to wait, listen, and respond. In this instance, the person may have an opinion about everything you just said. In fact, it's almost guaranteed that there will be opinions and possible anger because of your words. That's okay. You are focusing on the best decision for you and your overall well being.

Here's the deal: if you have decided that you are done, there doesn't have to be a back and forth on this. You do not have to remain in a relationship because you are more fearful of what the ending may be like versus staying in it. You can make a clean break.

We just learned that ending a relationship can be in your best interest. Yet still, you may wonder if you should end the relationship.

Or if the relationship already ended, do you attempt to restart it? I included a few questions to ponder about relational endings:

What relationships have I been involved in that have ended?

- Do I remember why it ended?
- What role did I play in the relationship ending?
- Was an ending the best choice for the relationship? Why or why not?

What relationships have ended that I may want to restart?

- Why do I want to restart them?
- How did the relationship benefit me?
- How do I think the other person will respond to a communication from me?

While these questions are not an exhaustive list of considerations for either ending or restarting a relationship, it is an anchor from which to start. You can identify your role in what happened and reflect on how you perceive the other person acted in the situation.

Toxic Communication Patterns

Even if you come to a decision about a relationship ending, you may still be unsure. Ending a relationship is a decision that will have downstream effects. You will move through life without this person, and that's a new space to experience. Sure, you may know you need to walk away, but comfort can keep you in it. Ease can keep you in it. Fear of life without the person, even if not ideal, can keep you in it. Yet still, there are indications that you may need to end the relationship. Earlier we learned about family communication patterns. Equally important to recognize are toxic communication patterns.

A pattern is something we become comfortable following even if it is harmful to us in some way. Just because a pattern seems normal does not mean it isn't damaging to our overall wellbeing. In terms of toxic communication patterns, think about how you feel after speaking with someone. After you communicate with the other person, do you feel bad? Is your confidence lowered a bit? Do you feel bullied or as if you have to brace yourself to defend what may be hurled at you during the conversation? These feelings and behaviors may be normal for you, but they are not healthy for you. In fact, they are toxic. Toxic communication patterns are also signs that you need to end a relationship.

Toxic relationships create communication land mines. This means the communication is unhealthy in some way for everyone involved and is highly volatile. Communicative messages are confusing, manipulative, hurtful, and abusive. Research by Dr. John Gottman tells us there are four communication styles, identified as the four horsemen, that are the most damaging to relationships over time. In fact, he predicts these four communication habits lead to divorce: criticism, defensiveness, contempt, and stonewalling. While we are not focused on marital relationships in this book, it is important to understand that these same four patterns may be just as destructive to friendships and families. Since communication can become a pattern, you can easily fall into a pattern of behaviors out of habit. Fortunately, you can change your habits. Let's look at each of the four toxic communication patterns.

Criticism is an expression of disapproval of someone or something based on perceived faults or mistakes. Criticism is often just thoughtlessness and inconsideration by another person, but it can also be deliberately malicious and hurtful. This can take the form of many things like pointing out (perceived) personality flaws and blaming. We may not realize that over time, criticism is detrimental to both the person hurling the criticism and the person being criticized. The person bearing the brunt of criticism can suffer from anger, resentment, frustration, depression, anxiety, and stress. Being on the receiving end of criticism long-term can wear us down and wear us out. We become emotionally drained. We doubt ourselves and our abilities. We feel like we can never live up to the approval of the other person. Our mind begins to repeat the things we are hearing (negative self-talk) and we begin to believe it.

The person delivering the criticism may be suffering with feelings of insecurity or, surprisingly, aggravation, because the person is most like the person they are criticizing. A fair amount of criticism is born from insecurity. When someone is not comfortable with themselves, they point out the faults and flaws of others. They attempt to make themselves feel better by making others feel worse. Criticism says more about the person doing the criticizing than the person to whom the critic is aimed. Think about it ... you probably have the most contention with the parent who is most like you. You likely get easily annoyed by the co-worker who does the things that you do. Criticism can be intentional or unintentional. Regardless of why we deliver or tolerate criticism, it is toxic to our ability to communicate with one another.

We have not touched on all the possible reasons why we may deliver criticism or suffer from it at the hand of others. But we do know that criticism does not lead people to change behavior. Instead, it creates anger and defensiveness on the part of the person criticized. Communication is hampered and positive relationships impeded. As we reflect on our experiences with criticism, these questions will help us think about if we should end or at the very least confront criticism in our lives.

Questions to ponder if I am criticized:

- What makes the criticism a pattern?
- How have I responded to the criticism?
- How can I respond to the criticism differently?

Questions to ponder if I am the one giving the criticism:

- Whenever I criticize someone, am I truly critiquing a situation or am I speaking from insecurity?

- Do I criticize because I am frustrated when someone acts exactly like me?
- Why does that bother me?

It makes sense for us to listen and consider the criticism. Specifically, we should consider the intent of the person who is criticizing. It is equally important to understand why we may accept criticism and from whom we are accepting it. When left unaddressed, criticism is toxic and detrimental to communication.

Defensiveness is self-protection in the form of righteous indignation or innocent victimhood to ward off a perceived attack. Many people become defensive when they are being criticized, but the problem is that its perceived effect is blame. Defensiveness is usually a counterattack to a complaint. When we feel threatened by verbal (tone of voice) or nonverbal (body language) communication, we tend to react or retaliate to defend ourselves. When we do that, we are less and less able to perceive accurately the other person's message and motive, because we are operating from a space of perception. If you recall, we discussed how dangerous perceptions can be because they are based on the perspective of one person without checking-in to see if the perspective is accurate.

When we feel threatened, we respond with a "fight or flight" response. In communication, the "fight" response is when we yell and argue. We use our tongues as weapons. These are signs that we do not feel emotionally safe. Yelling and aggression are triggered by perceptions, not the actual content of the communication. Flight is exactly what sounds like. We "check-out" of the communication. We can either leave physically or emotionally (stop listening), even if we are still physically present.

Being in a relationship where we feel we must protect ourselves from a verbal attack continuously is exhausting and unhealthy. Whether we are on the receiving end of someone complaining about us or our behavior, or we dish this out to others, here are some questions to reflect upon if ending a relationship.

Questions to ponder if I tend to defend myself in relationships:

- Which of my relationships have a pattern of defensive communication?
- What makes the communication defensive?
- How have I responded to the defensive communication?
- How can I respond to the defensiveness differently?

Questions to ponder if people defend themselves to me in relationships:

- How often is what I say judgmental or accusatory of another person?
- What are the motives behind what I say when folks get defensive in conversations with me?
- What are people most defending themselves from when in a conversation with me?
- How can I communicate differently so that others do not feel they have to defend themselves?

No doubt, defensiveness hinders the communication process and can result in a relationship ending. Whether we find ourselves defending ourselves or that people defend themselves to us often, we must admit that there is a problem that has taken a toll on the relationship and our wellbeing. If the problem has grown so great that we no longer enjoy the relationship, it should end.

Contempt is particularly dangerous because it conveys disgust, disdain, and disrespect. It is virtually impossible to overcome communication barriers when someone feels another person finds them disgusting. Contempt is fueled by long-simmering negative thoughts, and it attacks from a position of relative superiority. Make no mistake, contempt is a relationship ender. Whether in words or behaviors, contempt makes communication worse and either severely weakens or destroys relationships. Interestingly, the feelings are not really about the issues in the relationship; rather, they are an attack on the value of a person—almost like saying, "You are insignificant."

Contempt usually occurs when at least one person in the relationship can't express their anger or share why they're upset. Instead, they bottle up their feelings, which taints perspective and all communications. When there's contempt, it's near impossible to resolve conflict in a healthy way. That fact cannot be emphasized enough. Contempt destroys psychological, emotional, and physical health. It affects everything: communication, self-esteem, health, and wellbeing, creating a breeding ground for toxic behavior and communication patterns. It inevitably leads to more conflict and rarely, if ever, to a reset.

It is possible that you may feel contempt for someone or that someone has contempt for you, and you may not even know it. It's best to ask yourself a universal question, "Which of my relationships have characteristics of contempt (hostile humor and sarcasm, mockery, name-calling, mimicking, offensive body language [eye rolling, bullying, etc.])?"

That gets us in the mindset to tackle the next series of questions. Here are some questions to consider if contempt exists in a relationship:

Questions to ponder if I have contempt for someone:

- Who do I have contempt for?
- What is the source of the contempt?
- How should I best handle the relationship?

Questions to ponder if I feel someone has contempt for me:

- Who do I think might have feelings of contempt towards me?
- Why do I think this person has contempt for me?

- How have I responded to prior acts of contempt?

Contempt is a relationship killer. If there is evidence you show contempt towards someone or the other person has contempt for you, it is best to walk away. It is unreasonable to think that contempt just goes away—it doesn't. If it is present in a relationship, it will create persistent conflict. The ability to move forward is not likely.

Stonewalling is when we completely withdraw from interaction with someone else. If we are in a conversation with someone, it can take the form of closing ourselves off and completely stopping the interaction. It is also the continued refusal to interact with the other person. Some people use stonewalling as a coping mechanism to avoid conflict. Others may use this tactic intentionally to manipulate or control the other person. Regardless of the origin of stonewalling, it can have a detrimental impact on the communication process and subsequently the relationship.

For the person being stonewalled, it can leave them feeling confused, hurt, and angry. It can erode self-esteem, leading to feelings of worthlessness or hopelessness. For the person stonewalling, they suffer as they are denying themselves emotional connection with the other person. Despite which party starts stonewalling, it creates immense tension, makes an already strained relationship worse, and can lead to an end.

There are a few reasons why we stonewall others. One reason is that we are overwhelmed. It is easier for us to "vanish" emotionally than to be present and deal with the issues that cause us discomfort. Another reason is emotional suppression. It is easy to act like we are not feeling the emotions that are indeed present. The tricky part is that suppressed emotions do not merely go away because we act like they are not there. Those emotions that we think we have been able to hide always show up again, usually stronger than before. Another reason for stonewalling is to manipulate. This is the most toxic motive behind stonewalling in relationships because it is rooted in selfishness and borderline abusive.

Here's the deal: none of us want to walk a figurative communication tightrope, which is exactly what stonewalling requires us to do. Not only are we off balance, but we are also wading through the unknown, constantly wondering what is going on with the other person if someone is doing it to us. Equally, if we are the stonewaller, we are still left wondering what the other person thinks of the silence; is it [the manipulation] working?

Stonewalling is very common. In Dr. Gottman's lab, he found that approximately 85% of men use stonewalling as a method to quell conflict. This is not to say that women do not stonewall, because they do, but men tend to do it more often. But this is less about gender and more about the toxic behavior that bears the toxic communication pattern that ends relationships. When we stonewall, we are clearly disengaging from the person and the relationship. This psychological removal from relationships and situations results in disastrous fallout. If left unaddressed, stonewalling is likely to cause severe relational distress, conflict, and disruption. Even more, if we do not identify it and name it for what it is, it will pollute our overall wellbeing. Stonewalling can occur so often that we can discount it for "that's just how it is," which is why we should consider which relationships we are in that involve stonewalling. Here are some questions to consider about stonewalling:

Questions if I have stonewalled others:

- Who have I stonewalled?
- Why did I believe stonewalling was the best thing to do?
- What are other ways to respond besides stonewalling?

Questions to ponder if I have been stonewalled:

- How have others stonewalled me in relationships?
- How have I responded to acts of stonewalling from someone?

- How can I respond differently to being stonewalled by someone?

Stonewalling can be malicious, though it isn't always. No matter the origin of why someone is doing it, stonewalling is a toxic communication pattern. If you're able to recognize this behavior in yourself, then you are self-aware and emotionally mature. Acknowledging characteristics in yourself that may not represent your best self gives you strength and courage. Understanding that we need to change ourselves or end a relationship with someone who will not change is difficult to come to terms with, but growth is never easy. This is a moment to be proud of yourself.

A Time for Closure

When we think about ending relationships or restarting relationships, closure is always top of mind. For some reason, people feel that if they don't have closure on why somebody did something to them or why something ended the way it did, it is difficult to move on. But moving on without closure is indeed possible. Remember, I mentioned that we have to become comfortable with the uncomfortable. Well, this is one of those areas.

Closure, or something that we seek at the finality of a thing, is not someone else's responsibility necessarily. Typically, when we say, "I don't have closure" or "I need closure," we are placing the burden of closure, however we define it, onto someone or something else. For example, we may think, "But I need to know why you used to hit me when we were married." Or we may want to know, "Why did you ostracize me from the family when I came out as gay?" Or we may ask, "How could you just walk away from our family and start a whole new family with somebody else?"

Getting answers to these questions is important. As a matter of fact, getting answers to any lingering questions you may have about situations you feel were left open could be a part of the healing process. However, it is not THE healing process.

Your future does not depend on someone who did or did not give you closure. Sometimes people put great emphasis on the act of finally getting closure rather than the work they need to do to heal from the incident or from that season of life. Here's the truth about getting answers to these lingering questions: The answers you receive to your questions may not get you what you were hoping for. In other words, the answers you get can be broad, across-the-board, and positive or negative. You just don't know what you don't know. What if the answer to the question of "Why did you hit me when we were together?" is "because you do so many stupid things that you made me hit you"? Is that the closure you wanted? What if the answer to the question of "Why did you ostracize me from the family when I came out as gay?" is "I gave birth to a baby girl. I expected to walk you down the aisle, watch you get married to a man, and start a family in the traditional way. What am I supposed to tell people, my friends, the family? It's like you are ashamed of who you are; ashamed that God made you a girl. I don't understand any of this. This is too confusing for the family, for me, and for other people"? What if the answer to the question, "How could you just walk away from our family and start a whole new family with somebody else?" was "I was in a bad place in my life and did not want the added responsibility of taking care of a family. I could barely take care of me"?

Comparatively, responses could be more positive. For example, a response to the question of, "Why did you hit me when we were together?" might be, "I saw my dad hit my mom and I thought that is what you do to women in a relationship. I know it is not right and I'm sorry that I hit you." A response to the question of "Why did you ostracize me from the family when I came out as gay?" could be "I was so shocked at first, I really didn't know what to say or do. I was raised in a generation where being gay just wasn't an option. I know it was wrong to stop talking to you, but I am still dealing with all of this." Finally, the answer to the question, "How could you just walk away from our family and start a whole new family with somebody else?"

might be "It seemed like I couldn't do anything right and you all would be better without me. After some time, I made a better life for myself and then found love again. I did not plan it; it just happened."

Of the many possible outcomes, whether positive or negative, there could still be so many more questions generated from the seemingly final "closure conversation." You see, no matter how the person responds to any question you could possibly have, it still may not be enough. You could still be left feeling as if you don't have closure, and in no better position than before.

What we really want from closure is for something to be said that will remove our pain associated with the incident. We want someone to say something to make what happened make sense. We want to hear a reason for why they did something. We want them to return to the scene of the crime, if you will. That is an impossible and unfair task to ask of anyone. Sure, they may give reasons and try to make you understand their perspective, but could they ever say anything to undo the feelings and emotions you experienced when it happened? Of course not. Could they say anything that would rationalize what they did? No. You fundamentally cannot fathom why they would do it in the first place. How could they hurt you the way they did? So many questions go along with an issue that is left unresolved. That's why you have to make peace with moving on without getting closure from another person.

Closure is a personal decision. It is not about the other person. It is about you being able to move on from a situation with peace. In short, closure is your responsibility, not someone else's. Therefore, you need to define what closure means to you. You must decide exactly what you need for closure. When I mention what is needed, I mean what is within your control. Again, you cannot make anyone do anything. Furthermore, closure should be a process that you are able to move through with or without the other person.

Ending a relationship does not require you to have "the closure conversation" in order to move on. Don't hold yourself or the other person hostage to what still needs to be said. Moving on is about you being able to see the situation for what it was, identifying the part that everyone played, reflecting on how the situation affected your life, and recognizing how that experience is a part of who you are. It does not define you; it is simply a part of you. You are a better person because of it.

Endings Can Be Beginnings

Remember, it's okay for some relationships to end. Everyone we encounter or are related to may not be destined to be in our life forever—maybe just for a season or a particular reason. And that's okay. Also realize that ending a relationship can feel like a loss. That's because it is. Ending a relationship can indeed cause feelings of grief. And that's okay. The grieving process will be different for everyone and will occur over a different timeline for everyone. However, a loss is not always a loss, at least in the way we may think of it. Losing someone in your life is just that. It's an act that is independent of you. It does not define you. You are not a loser because you are experiencing a loss. The ending of a relationship can be a win. Deciding to end a relationship because it was no longer serving you or the person well means you made the best decision for your overall wellbeing. And gaining freedom in this way is priceless.

CHAPTER 8

The Beginning of Your Next Steps

"…we've been led to believe that communication is simple. But if it's so simple, how do so many of us get to a point in relationships where we don't know how to interact with a friend or family member anymore?"

Those are the words that I stated in Chapter 1. The reality is everyone has experienced some form of pain, disappointment, and discomfort from not addressing a taboo issue that has invaded a relationship. Most of us respond in negative, non-helpful ways. In fact, most of our knee-jerk reactions are the absolute wrong thing to do or say. Many of us revert to individual workarounds to mask the issue, or we learn to just live with it. Unfortunately, these approaches leave things unresolved, allowing them to fester over time. Time alone does not heal. Ignoring the issue does not heal. Ghosting the person does not heal. Suffering in silence does not heal.

When a taboo topic is present, when we carry shame about something that happened, or when we are ashamed of someone we are close to, communication is difficult. We carry the weight of those taboos in the way we engage with each other. As I hope you have discovered as you worked through the areas in this book, you don't have to settle for the dysfunction that has become normalized in relationships. You now have the tools and are building the skills to increase your confidence, take control of what you communicate to others, and guide what you receive from others. You are now equipped to establish a new normal and can take the best next steps for yourself and your wellbeing.

Your Best Next Steps

All the skills you learned about will not create instant success. You will not magically tackle a taboo topic that has plagued your life for months, years, or decades. It simply doesn't work that way. What does work is your ability to apply what you have learned. You develop skills through practice. The more often you apply the skills, the more they become habits, and the more they become a part of your internal default settings. Think about something you started out doing by writing a list of the steps or referencing a manual. In time and with repeated application, all the steps became a habit. This follows the same principle.

The skills that you learned will position you to navigate the next steps with confidence. When applying the skills, you will inevitably encounter a few challenges along the way; that is part of the process, so accept it moving forward. But also accept that you can do this, and you are a better person for embracing this process. You may feel discouraged at times. In fact, others may not grasp exactly what you are trying to do and might dismiss you or argue with you about the issue. You then have a choice: you can give up, give in, or stay the course. Given the work you have done so far, you can confidently stay the course, despite what you see in front of you. You are greater than the possible obstacles that will come along your path.

A lot of the issues we addressed in this book are difficult to handle and you still may have reservations about where to start. I mean, if you decided that you should stop being in a relationship with your mother, that is a tough call to make. If you learned that you stonewall others and need to stop doing it, that is difficult to come to terms with. If you discovered that you have trust issues in a relationship that you thought was secure, that can be overwhelming. Even with all these truths lingering, you have the power and the ability to establish communication with another person in a way that frees you from hiding. No one should function in a relationship with issues covered up. Tear off the covers!

You are already winning because you have taken the time to

devote to improving your communication skills. You have learned so much about yourself and those close to you. Remember that communication flows along a continuum and therefore is a life-long learning process. We are all always learning how to communicate and not simply talk with another person. We are all always communicating as others are making decisions and judgments about each of us based on what they perceive. It is our responsibility to ensure the communication is accurate and reflective of our truth.

All of this comes down to a few points: 1) recognize communication patterns; 2) identify your role in the communication; and 3) explore how you can communicate differently. That is what this is all about. You have realized the potential of your communication skills. That's important. Your potential has no bounds.

Learning how to communicate is like building muscle. You gain strength in your communication skills every time you use them. With each "practice session," you are adding more weight to your workout. In order to know how strong the muscle is becoming over time, you must check on the progress. Ask people. This is not an "I gotcha" moment; rather, it's an opportunity to learn more about how another person perceives you and your behaviors. Remember, someone's perception of you tells you more about them than it does about you.

Communication is an asset we all have. You just need to unpack all of its benefits. As you do, always remember that what is in front of you is greater than what is behind you. Keep moving forward on your communication journey. Own your communication.

NOTES

Sillars AL. Interpersonal conflict. The handbook of communication science. 2010:273-290.

Cupach WR, Canary DJ, Spitzberg BH. Competence in interpersonal conflict: Waveland Press 2009.

Terhune KW. Motives, situation, and interpersonal conflict within Prisoner's Dilemma. Journal of personality and social psychology. 1968;8(3p2):1.

Boyes AD, Latner JD. Weight stigma in existing romantic relationships. Journal of Sex & Marital Therapy. 2009;35(4):282-293.

Schulze B. Stigma and mental health professionals: A review of the evidence on an intricate relationship. International review of Psychiatry. 2007;19(2):137-155.

Link BG, Phelan JC. Conceptualizing Stigma. Annual Reviews Inc 2001:363

Ong LM, De Haes JC, Hoos AM, et al. Doctor-patient communication: a review of the literature. Social science & medicine. 1995;40(7):903-918.

Pendleton D, Schofield T, Tate P, et al. The new consultation: developing doctor-patient communication: OUP Oxford 2003.

Calafell BM, Chuang S, Cooks L, et al. Critical intercultural communication pedagogy: Lexington Books 2017.

Segrin C, Flora J. Family communication: Routledge 2018

Galvin KM, Braithwaite DO, Bylund CL. Family communication: Cohesion and change: Routledge 2015.

Austen J, Lynch D. Persuasion: Oxford University Press 2008

Cozby PC. Self-disclosure: A literature review. Psychological bulletin. 1973;79(2):73-91

Derlega VJ, Metts S, Petronio S, et al. Self-disclosure: Sage Publications, Inc 1993

Petronio S. Boundaries of privacy: Dialectics of disclosure: Suny Press 2002

Why Relationships Go Bad

Noelle-Neumann E. The spiral of silence a theory of public opinion. Journal of communication. 1974;24(2):43-51.

Jay T. The utility and ubiquity of taboo words. Perspectives on psychological science. 2009;4(2):153-161.

Jay KL, Jay TB. Taboo word fluency and knowledge of slurs and general pejoratives: Deconstructing the poverty-of-vocabulary myth. Language Sciences. 2015;52:251-259

Faux M. Roe v. Wade: the untold story of the landmark Supreme Court decision that made abortion legal: Cooper Square Press 2000.

Ginsburg RB. Some thoughts on autonomy and equality in relation to Roe v. Wade. NCL Rev. 1984;63:375.

Rapoport I. Thoughts on the overturn of Roe vs. Wade.

Hull N, Hoffer PC. Roe v. Wade: The abortion rights controversy in American history: University Press of Kansas 2010.

Ellis C, Flaherty MG. Investigating subjectivity: Research on lived experience: Sage 1992.

Mohr J, Spekman R. Characteristics of partnership success: partnership attributes, communication behavior, and conflict resolution techniques. Strategic management journal. 1994;15(2):135-152.

Putnam LL. Definitions and approaches to conflict and communication. The Sage handbook of conflict communication: Integrating theory, research, and practice. 2006:1-32.

Berger CR, Roloff ME. Interpersonal communication. An integrated approach to communication theory and research: Routledge 2019:277-292

McCornack S. Reflect and relate: Bedford Bks St Martin's 2010

Long, N., Long, J., & Whitson, S. (2008). The angry smile. Austin, TX: Pro-Ed.

Warren R. The purpose driven life: What on earth am I here for?: Zondervan 2012.

Hart K. Laugh at My Pain: Code Black Entertainment 2012.

Rock C. Chris Rock: Bring the Pain: Dreamworks Records 1996

Fields R. Drugs in perspective: Brown & Benchmark 1995.

Cultivate a Communication Mindset

Chapman G, Campbell R. The 5 Love Languages/5 Love Languages for Men/5 Love Languages of Teenagers/5 Love Languages of Children: Moody Publishers 2016.

"Talk." Merriam-Webster.com Dictionary, Merriam-Webster, https://www.merriam-webster.com/dictionary/talk. Accessed 11 Aug. 2022.

"Communication." Merriam-Webster.com Dictionary, Merriam-Webster, https://www.merriam-webster.com/dictionary/communication. Accessed 11 Aug. 2022.

Dember WN. The psychology of perception. 1960.

Watzlawick P, Beavin J, Jackson D. Some tentative axioms of communication. Communication theory: Routledge 2017:74-80.

"Meet Doctor Nowzaradan". Houston Obesity Surgery. Retrieved 10 Aug. 2022.

Lakoff G. The meanings of literal. Metaphor and Symbol. 1986;1(4):291-296.

Giora R. On the priority of salient meanings: Studies of literal and figurative language. Journal of pragmatics. 1999;31(7):919-929

Finfgeld TE, DeVito JA, Murphy R, et al. The ability to select words to convey intended meaning. Quarterly Journal of Speech. 1966;52(3):255-258.

Olson DR. Language and thought: aspects of a cognitive theory of semantics. Psychological review. 1970;77(4):257.

Resolve the Tensions that Permeate Your Relationships

Segrin C, Flora J. Family communication: Routledge 2018.

Remove the Roadblocks to Effective Communication

Bereby-Meyer Y, Shalvi S. Deliberate honesty. Current Opinion in Psychology. 2015;6:195-198.

McCroskey JC. The communication apprehension perspective. Avoiding communication: Shyness, reticence, and communication apprehension. 1984:13-38.

Jung MH, Moon A, Nelson LD. Overestimating the valuations and preferences of others. J Exp Psychol Gen. 2020;149(6):1193-1214

"Judgment." Merriam-Webster.com Dictionary, Merriam-Webster, https://www.merriam-webster.com/dictionary/judgment. Accessed 12 Aug. 2022.

Link BG, Phelan JC. Conceptualizing Stigma. Annual Reviews Inc 2001:363.

Coleman LM. Stigma. The dilemma of difference: Springer 1986:211-232.

Turner JC. Social influence: Thomson Brooks/Cole Publishing Co 1991.

Raven BH. Social influence and power. California Univ Los Angeles 1964.

Broderick CB. Understanding family process: Basics of family systems theory: Sage 1993.

Koerner AF, Fitzpatrick MA. Family communication patterns theory: A social cognitive approach. Engaging theories in family communication: Multiple perspectives. 2006:50-65.

Wilmot W, Hocker JL. Interpersonal conflict: McGraw-Hill Education 2017.

Develop the Courage to Communicate About the Tension

"Courage." Merriam-Webster.com Dictionary, Merriam-Webster, https://www.merriam-webster.com/dictionary/courage. Accessed 12 Aug. 2022.

Goud NH. Courage: Its nature and development. The Journal of Humanistic Counseling, Education and Development. 2005;44(1):102-116.

Afifi TD, Afifi WA. Uncertainty, information management, and disclosure decisions : theories and applications: New York : Routledge, 2009 2009.

McKnight DH, Chervany NL. The meanings of trust. 1996.

Rempel JK, Holmes JG, Zanna MP. Trust in close relationships. Journal of personality and social psychology. 1985;49(1):95.

The Relationship Reset

Cloud H, Townsend J. Boundaries updated and expanded edition: When to say yes, how to say no to take control of your life: Zondervan 2017

Cloud H, Townsend J. Boundaries in marriage: Zondervan 2002.

Cloud H, Townsend JS, Guest L. Boundaries with Kids: When to Say Yes, when to Say No to Help Your Children Gain Control of Their Lives: Zondervan 1998

Spataro SE, Bloch J. "Can you repeat that?" Teaching active listening in management education. Journal of Management Education. 2018;42(2):168-198

Pillemer K. Fault lines: Fractured families and how to mend them: Penguin 2020.

When It's Time to Walk Away

Schoppe-Sullivan SJ, Coleman J, Wang J, et al. Mothers' attributions for estrangement from their adult children. Couple and Family Psychology: Research and Practice. 2021.

Gottman JM. Gottman method couple therapy. Clinical handbook of couple therapy. 2008;4(8):138-164.

Levenson RW, Gottman JM. Physiological and affective predictors of change in relationship satisfaction. Journal of personality and social psychology. 1985;49(1):85.

Research FAQs. (n.d.). Frequently asked questions about Dr. Gottman's research. Retrieved from http://www.gottman.com/49853/Research-FAQs.html

ABOUT THE AUTHOR

Dr. Demetria McNeal is a communication scientist, academic researcher, popular speaker, corporate trainer, and communication coach. She helps individuals, executives, entrepreneurs, health care institutions, and health care clinicians dismantle communication pitfalls that stifle relationships, create disparities in health outcomes, derail health interventions, and impede organizational progress. Her unique perspective and experiences on how communication affects the individual and greater health care milieu leads to provocative solutions to wicked problems.

Demetria is renowned for her fun, highly interactive, and engaging presentations, and her ability to help consulting clients own their communication. She is also a keynote speaker, wife, bonus mom, and writer at demetriamcnealauthor.com.